POLITICS AND NATIONHOOD

POLITICS AND NATIONHOOD

Post-Revolutionary Portugal

Thomas C. Bruneau

PRAEGER SPECIAL STUDIES • PRAEGER SCIENTIFIC

New York • Philadelphia • Eastbourne, UK
Toronto • Hong Kong • Tokyo • Sydney

Library of Congress Cataloging in Publication Data

Bruneau, Thomas C.
  Politics and nationhood.

  Bibliography: p.
  Includes index.
  1. Portugal—Politics and government—1974–
I. Title.
DP681.B78   1984   946.9′044   83-17784
ISBN 0-03-069464-7 (alk. paper)

Published in 1984 by Praeger Publishers
CBS Educational and Professional Publishing
a Division of CBS Inc.
521 Fifth Avenue, New York, NY 10175 USA

3456789   052   987654321

Printed in the United States of America
on acid-free paper

For Madame Goldstein
Proprietor of York House in Lisbon

Preface

The importance of developments in Portugal since the military coup of April 25, 1974, cannot be overemphasized, for Portugal itself, and is equally significant for students of comparative and international politics. Portugal is the world's oldest nation-state with the same boundaries and was once one of the most advanced maritime powers. From its high point in the fifteenth and sixteenth centuries, however, the country has been surpassed economically and socially by other nations—not only in Europe and North America, but even by some industrializing countries in the Third World. In 1974 Portugal was the longest lived non-Communist dictatorship and the only self-acknowledged corporatist state. It was also unwilling to relinquish control of the last colonial empire. The coup of April 25 brought all of this to an end and gave Portugal the chance to catch up rapidly with other European nations. The dictatorship and corporatist state has given way to the gradual, if uneven, establishment of a liberal democratic regime with a diversity of groups and political parties and a Constitution stating progressive goals for the country. In place of the colonial empire the country has embarked on a campaign to enter Europe, and specifically, the European Economic Community. In simplest terms, Portugal since 1974 has been attempting to modernize after a very long period of backwardness and isolation from trends and processes characterizing the modern world. This process of modernization is by no means completed, and there are a great many difficult problems yet to be confronted and resolved. The experience itself is extremely interesting not only for those concerned with Portugal, but also for students of modernization, revolution, political change, and the formation of regimes.

Yet the case of Portugal holds more than purely academic interest. The rapid demise of the Portuguese "Estado Novo" on April 25 and the tenuous but continuing process of consolidation of a new regime presaged the demise of other authoritarian regimes but with widely differing results, as illustrated by the cases of Spain, Iran, and Nicaragua. After a long period of military coups and the formation of authoritarian regimes throughout the Third World, it appears that the trend has been reversed, whether permanently or not, with the liberalization or democratization of military regimes in Latin America and sub-Saharan Africa. Portugal, as the first case, bears examining for the lessons it may hold for other countries currently undergoing democratization. One of the most encouraging characteristics of the change in Portugal has been the extremely low level of violence: fewer than one hundred people have been killed in politically motivated acts during the period 1974–81, a statistic that is doubly remarkable in view of the fact that the country was then absorbing more than a half million refugees from the newly-independent colonies. Portugal has avoided the vengeful violence of the "pied noir" in France, the regional violence in Spain, the civil war in Nicaragua, and the religious fanaticism in Iran. What is more, in November 1979 a general amnesty was declared restoring full political rights to those involved in illegal political actions, both Left and Right. One would hope that there is something to be learned from the Portuguese experience of a largely nonviolent revolution that can be applied elsewhere.

In Portugal in 1974 elements in the military, tired of fighting hopeless wars to retain the colonies, instituted the change of regime. In their program, the Armed Forces Movement (MFA) promised to decolonize, democratize, and develop the country, particularly for the benefit of the lower classes. To a surprisingly high degree, this has succeeded. Thus the military, in contrast to other periods in Portuguese history and the experience of the vast majority of other countries, intervened from the Left with progressive goals which were not subsequently ignored in the struggle for power. In contrast to another case of progressive military intervention—Peru, 1968–78—the Portuguese military did not seek to retain power, but rather through a complex and at times contradictory process, established a civilian regime with a gradually decreasing military involvement. And, in contrast to another potentially similar case, Cuba, the progressive military were but briefly influenced by the Communist Party (PCP) despite the fact that for a period in 1975 it appeared as though this party was seeking power.

While avoiding the experience of Cuba, the Portuguese also side-stepped the more probable experience of Chile in 1973. The post-1974 provisional governments included members of the PCP, and for a period in 1975 there was indeed great political instability. However, contrary to suggestions on the part of elements both within and without Portugal, foreigners did not directly intervene to remove the Left from power. The role of the United States was cautious and reasonable, representing a substantial change from its involvement in Chile. This rational approach was at least partially due to the heavy involvement of European countries, most notably the Federal Republic of Germany, in the resolution of the threat of Leftist ascendance in Portugal. Seen for the first time since the end of World War II was the application of not only the economic but also the political influence of Germany. The Germans, the Socialist International, and finally the European Economic Community all became involved in assisting a particular resolution to the political crises in Portugal.

The singularity of the Portuguese case has been largely due to the political involvement and even integration of Portuguese groups, parties, and institutions with counterparts in Europe and North America. These include unions, research institutes, political parties, financial institutions, and the military. The purpose, at times coordinated and at other times not, of these foreign actors has been to include Portugal economically, politically, and militarily in a "Western system" thereby avoiding both the threat of Communism and the return to the old, Rightist, regime. The pattern of modernization in Portugal since the coup of 1974, then, has been in part determined by the intentional integration with a great variety of actors in other, more modern, and richer countries. The most important question, now that the issue of the political regime is apparently resolved, is the kind of economy and society likely to result from the economic integration, significant before 1974 but now greatly accelerated, which is implied with the planned inclusion in the European Economic Community. Will the positive implications of the political and military integration be somehow negated if Portugal's role on the periphery of the more advanced European economies is further consolidated? Or, will the terms of integration (political and economic) allow for a renegotiation of Portugal's backward situation? To the constraints likely to be imposed by accession to the EEC must be added those of the democratic system itself. Given the cultural background of the Portuguese people, which was exacerbated during the almost half a century of the Salazar regime, the population is generally conservative in sociopolitical attitudes. During the revolutionary period and into 1976 a number of models of society and economy were proposed, and the Constitution of 1976 enshrined a fairly advanced one in the basic charter of the country. However, since 1976 it has become clear to some political groups that the Constitution is inappropriate to their image of Portugal, and they are changing it. What was achieved through revolution is now being negotiated through electoral politics, and this in a context of international constraints due not only to recession but also to the multiple links arising from the small size of Portugal today and the involvements initiated with the revolution.

The purpose of this book is to analyze the formation of the regime in Portugal since 1974. My data base for this attempt is broad and rich. I became interested in the country in the early 1960s and visited twice as a tourist. It was in the summer of 1973 that I first conducted research there on the relationship of Church and state. At that time I spent two months and became fascinated with the obvious changes taking place in economy and society. By then I had already joined a group of North American social scientists interested in Portugal, which met for the first time in 1972 and founded the International Conference Group on Modern Portugal and held an international conference in the fall of 1973.[1] This provided an excellent opportunity to come into contact with Portuguese researchers, and to get a sense of the drama unfolding after twelve years of wars in Africa and the intransigence of a regime which would not admit to negotiation and severely restricted political debate. Having done a draft of an article on Church and state, I returned to Portugal in the spring of 1974 for more interviews and an elaboration of what I felt to be an incomplete analysis. I was thus in Portugal on April 25, 1974, and had the opportunity to see and experience the revolution firsthand. For a political scientist with an academic background in the study of revolution, a research background in the country itself, a command of the language, and a number of contacts from the past summer's research and the international conference, it was a felicitious event for me as a researcher as well as for the Portuguese people. I thus decided to "acompanhar" (monitor) events and ultimately write a book dealing with the revolution and the regime emerging from it. Little did I know then that by the time I wrote the book there would have been six provisional governments and another eight under the Constitution of 1976, as well as attempted coups from the Right and Left, ascendance of the PCP, the possibility of foreign intervention, and a high level of political involvement by the population.

From the first days after April 25 I developed a joint project to study the post-revolutionary developments with a Portuguese colleague and friend from the previous year, Dr. Mário Bacalhau. On my part this involved an attempt to relate social science concepts to events there, and on his the collection of materials: newspapers, party documents, drafts of political platforms and constitutions, public opinion research, and so on, whereby together we could formulate an overall view of political dynamics. I was able to return to Portugal only in September of 1975 as I was conducting research in Brazil in the intervening period. I then returned in the summer of 1976, November of 1976, February of 1977, October of 1978, September of 1979, fall of 1981, and spring of 1982 to collect materials, conduct interviews, and work with Dr. Bacalhau. We were able to carry out a major national sample survey in March of 1978 to gauge popular attitudes on the results of the revolution and the new regime(s). In addition to extensive interviews in Portugal, and in many cases interviews which were repeated year after year, I also conducted interviews in Brussels, Bonn, New York, and Washington. This research—interviews, the sample survey, and in conjunction with the tremendous amount of documentation collected by Dr. Bacalhau and my own collection of books and weekly newspapers—was to provide a basis for the analysis contained in the rest of this book.

It was admittedly frustrating not to have written this book sooner. It was probably for the best that I did delay for it has taken these nine years for the regime to become defined in what is apparently a reasonably clear, albeit unstable pattern. With these years, and the distance this implies, I have the sense that my analysis pertains to an ongoing system and not one likely to be overthrown before this book is published.

It is impossible to thank individually all those who have assisted me in coming to understand Portuguese politics. Many of the scholars involved in the International Conference Group on Modern Portugal have provided stimulation, support, information, and contacts. Mário Bacalhau is but the most helpful of some 60 Portuguese who individually spent hours over the years talking about their country. Another dozen high level officials in five embassies in Lisbon gave freely of their time and informaton. I was well treated in all of the capitals and have in particular relied on my German colleagues for information. My colleagues at McGill assisted with the formulation of the questionnaire, which was well-administered by NORMA under the supervision of Mário Bacalhau. Drafts of my papers have circulated to colleagues, and these papers as well as the present manuscript have benefited from their comments and suggestions. For the present manuscript, I am particularly grateful to Professors Alex Macleod, José Medeiros Ferreira, and Walter Opello for their comments and criticisms. In sum, I was greatly assisted by well-informed participants and scholars at all stages of this project, and if the manuscript does not meet their expectations I must accept the blame for not repaying them for their time and interest.

I was able to conduct this research with support from the Social Science Research Subcommittee of McGill University, the Inter-University Centre for European Studies of Montreal, the Rockefeller Foundation in their program on Conflict in International Relations, and the Social Sciences and Humanities Research Council of Canada. The manuscript has been typed by Cathy Duggan and Judy Warnock. To them I also extend my thanks.

Obviously the collection of such a wide variety of data and other assorted materials over a period of nine years has resulted in a vast accumulation of information. My purpose here is not to disseminate all this information, as the result would be a very long book indeed. Rather, I have opted for a synopsis which highlights the most important themes and developments in order to understand the most recent process of regime-formation. While citing widely, then, I will be extremely selective in providing descriptive materials which may be found in the sources cited as well as in the bibliography. If there is an aspiring historian interested in writing a descriptive history of this period my files are open.

Note

1. For a discussion on the background and development of the ICGMP see the introduction in Lawrence Graham and Harry M. Makler (eds.), *Contemporary Portugal: The Revolution and Its Antecedents* (Austin: University of Texas Press, 1979).

Contents

Introduction: Themes in the Literature and Conceptual Approach

In light of the fascinating and important political developments in Portugal since 1974, the analytical political science
literature available to assist one in understanding the experience is weak. Portugal itself has seen a great outpouring of
material, but such material is generally most useful in providing facts, data, and personal views on the events and processes
initiated with the coup of April 25, 1974. The memoirlike
books by political actors such as Otelo Saraiva de Carvalho,
Mário Soares, and António de Spínola are very useful for insights into the thinking of those involved in politics, but do not
really seek to analyze objectively the actual process of the revolution. The immediate history books, best represented by the
three written by Avelino Rodrigues, and associates, again provide tremendous documentation but are both lacking in analytical frameworks (for the authors are journalists) and
somewhat biased by the proximity of the authors to one individual or group (in this case to Otelo Saraiva de Carvalho).
There are a great many service books which provide material
on institutions such as the constitution and the government,
processes such as elections, and groups such as political parties and unions. With these we can better understand the components of the political system, but they in themselves do not
seek to link the various components. There is much good material on the economy and agrarian reform; however, these publications do not normally provide much of a political perspective
and tend to remain specifically-focused. The analytical articles in journals such as *Análise Social* and *Economia e Socialismo* are frequently excellent, but extremely specific.

1

Missing in the above is a middle-level approach in which the details are integrated and structures and processes analyzed. The details and the perspectives are available in the Portuguese literature, but not the integration. This absence is perfectly understandable if we recall that the social sciences were discouraged under the old regime. The few academics who did work in this field, normally while in exile, were in great demand for political and administrative positions after the revolution and were thus too busy to write analysis since they were fully occupied developing tactics in the political struggle. Now, with a certain sifting out of the political elites, a number of these foreign-trained social scientists such as António Barreto, Manuel Lucena, and José Medeiros Ferreira are beginning to produce excellent studies. In the meantime one could not do much better than the essays of political analysis found in such weekly newspapers as *Expresso* and *O Jornal*. In the absence of an established social science the more perceptive political journalists provide elements for an analysis of political developments in Portugal. However, by virtue of journalism it must deal with specific events and is consequently less concerned with the analysis of long-run trends and processes. In sum, there is a great abundance of material in Portuguese from memoirs to service books to immediate history to journalism, all of which serves to provide the basis for an analysis of the situation since 1974. There is not at this time any single study which brings this material together in an analytical manner for an understanding of what happened and why.

The literature by foreigners on Portugal since the revolution is best described as mixed in quality. The problems facing the foreign analyst are many, and the following are but the most obvious. Few, whether they were academics or journalists, had any background in Portugal, and therefore lacked an historical perspective that could only be obtained through a great investment of time and energy; most were not interested in making this commitment as events were changing quite rapidly and the relevance of the past was not immediately obvious. Revolutions are inherently controversial and lend themselves to ideological and even polemical interpretations; as there were few poles or axes on which analysis could be centered the analyst could give free reign to imagination. This was aggravated by the fact that many of those drawn by Portugal have very clear political commitments and were writing less as objective observers and more in line with their political commitments and party affiliations. To say that this material is mixed is not to deny its merits and insights, but generally it adds little to what the Portuguese themselves have produced when it should have provided an added and objective dimension for critical reflection within the country. Aspiring Portuguese social scientists have discovered that much of this foreign-produced material is no less biased and no more perceptive than analyses produced at home, a discovery which has had a salutary effect on their self-image.

Some further and more specific comment is required concerning the literature to which I am referring. Rather than review all the articles in scholarly journals (which would then necessitate a review of articles in prestigious newspapers such as *Le Monde, The Guardian Weekly,* and the New York *Times*), I will limit myself to some comments on books that have appeared as these are indicative of the types of materials and the merits and difficulties.* The literature that claims to be academic, and thus presumably objective and analytical, is very limited in quantity. What with the competing demands on academics and the delays in publishing through academic presses this fact is easily understood. A relatively recent book is edited by Jorge Braga de Macedo and Simon Serfaty and entitled *Portugal Since the Revolution: Economic and Political Perspectives.* The book is mainly concerned with economics, however, and the main essay on politics is written by the present author, although the two commentaries on my essay are quite good. The other three essays and commentaries are also interesting, but are not concerned with explaining the processes and implications of the revolution in the political realm. The book does not seek to integrate the essays beyond the use of commentaries. A more complete and varied collection is that edited by Lawrence Graham and Harry Makler, *Contemporary Portugal: The Revolution and Its Antecedents.* It includes essays on many important aspects of pre- and post-revolutionary Portugal, which are dealt with from a number of disciplinary perspectives. It has the strengths of any collected work in that it provides a variety of approaches and themes. However, it lacks any particular integrating theme beyond the focus on Portugal (with a discussion on the study of Portugal as well in the excellent Preface and Introduction), and more se-

---

*For listings of bibliographies as well as specific books and articles see the bibliography.

riously for my purposes, does not deal systematically with questions of regime-formation since the revolution. There is very little concern with international dimensions of the revolution and little discussion of structural change. Clearly, the strength of this book lies with its analysis of the old regime, although it does provide some elements to understand what followed 1974. The new volume edited by Lawrence Graham and Douglas Wheeler, *In Search of Modern Portugal*, fills a number of gaps, but again the degree of integration, despite the excellent Introduction by Joyce Riegelhaupt, is limited as the book was also based on conference papers, and not prepared with an integrating theme.

Douglas Porch has written *The Portuguese Armed Forces and the Revolution* which promised to be an important contribution to the study of the military and their role in the revolution. The book is, however, disappointing as it is based on little original research in archives or through interviews, and is partisan in favor of the Socialist Party (PS). Porch pays particular attention to the internal career dynamics of the military, and while this perspective is useful for the background to the coup it loses its utility as all society became involved in revolutionary dynamics with the consequent politicization of the military itself. The goals of the author were apparently quite limited and by relying heavily on material dealing with the French military in Algeria, he failed to develop a noticeable understanding of the Portuguese revolution. Three early books on the revolution are those of Neil Bruce (*Portugal: The Last Empire*), Rhona Fields (*The Portuguese Revolution and the Armed Forces Movement*), and Mikael Harsgor (*Naissance d'un Nouveau Portugal*). The first deals mainly with the period before the coup and contains many factual errors which may decrease one's confidence in the overall analysis. The second book also contains many errors indicating little previous research experience in Portugal. Her analysis relies heavily on the interpretations of her informants with apparently little outside corroboration. She failed to verify what she wrote and rather published it in a form that can only cause embarrassment today. Harsgor's book is somewhat poetic and is very sensitive to the dynamics of the revolution. Its main deficiency lies in the fact that its completion made it unable to take into consideration the fundamental changes brought about by the frustrated Leftist coup of November 25, 1975. All in all, the academic literature on Portugal has been limited and is not particularly good. At the present there are a few German scholars writing books on the topic which promise to add to our knowledge of the revolution and the aftermath. Unfortunately, I am unable to read German and thus cannot comment on these books until I either have them read or they are translated. I feel it is indicative, however, that many of the most promising books are in fact being written in Germany rather than in North America. This is suggestive of the varying relevance of the topic between the two geographical areas as well as the current availability of resources for research.[1]

The overwhelming majority of books on Portuguese politics have a clear political orientation (in the sense of party affiliation) or are journalistic; in many cases these two characteristics are combined. Undoubtedly the best book in the genre of journalism is Antonio de Figueiredo's *Portugal: Fifty Years of Dictatorship.* It is mainly concerned with the background to the revolution, but includes as well pertinent observations on the first year and a half after April 25. Figueiredo is Portuguese but lives in England and combines a nice commitment to Portugal with a certain objectivity and distance from living abroad. This book is a contribution both to an understanding of Portugal and to its Portuguese author. Also of high quality is the book by the Insight Team of the Sunday Times, *Insight on Portugal: The Year of the Captains.* It provides a good running account of the first year and a half of the revolution combined with a certain amount of background information. Its main drawback, as with Harsgor's and Figueiredo's, is that it was completed in the fall of 1975 and thus cannot include the fundamental shifts brought about by November 25. Even so, the perspective is sufficiently broad that the event and reactions to it could have been anticipated. The same cannot be said of Marcio Moreira Alves' *Les Soldats Socialistes du Portugal* for his commitment to the more radical of the "soldiers in power" is quite clear and the book's virtue of providing a good deal of information is counterbalanced by its bias and does not prepare us for the demise of the Armed Forces Movement (MFA) and the eclipse of the radicals after November 25. A book by another journalist is Robert Harvey's *Portugal: Birth of a Democracy,* which brings the discussion up until early 1978. The author could draw upon his experience with the *Economist* and is thus strong on interviews and

"insider information." The author's opinions are all too obvious throughout the text, and there are no footnotes or bibliography for further support.

The other available books are more clearly politically-com-
mitted, and this has implications for the quality and objectivity of the presentation. Of course some of the academics (as in
the case of Bruce) demonstrate sympathy with the Right, and
journalists with both sides (Alves to the Left and Harvey to the
Center-Right), but we can give them the benefit of the doubt
and assume they are primarily interested in describing. Probably the best book by a clearly politically committed author is
Phil Mailer's *Portugal: The Impossible Revolution?* where his
anarchist perspective serves him well in allowing us to appreciate the spontaneity and involvement of the people ("O Povo")
and the less than consistent and positive role of the PCP. This
is a marvelous book to read in seeking a sense of the percep-
tions and reactions of those involved at the lower levels of society, although not necessarily at the lowest. There is little on
the elite and it is not a complete book in any sense of the term.
Jacques Frémontier's *Portugal: Les Points sur les i* is good
possibly because of his past membership in the French Communist Party; the author is able to perceive and criticize the
role of the PCP from the inside, a situation which does not apply to Harvey and Mailer. His analysis is stronger for during
the events described in the book the PCF did not criticize (as
did the Italian Communist Party) the strategy pursued by the
PCP. It too provides a running account of the first two years of
the revolution, but in my view its main strength is the author's
particular vantage point from within a sister party. The books
by other politically committed authors have less to recommend them. Wilfred Burchett's *Portugal Depois da Revolução
dos Capitães* is anecdotal, and one learns more about his political opinions than the topics he is ostensibly concerned with.
Jean Pierre Faye, the editor of *Portugal: The Revolution in the
Labyrinth,* might have been much more useful if he was more
critical of many of the views of one of the key participants—
Otelo Saraiva de Carvalho. In any case Otelo has written his
own books, the most important of which is *Alvorada em Abril,*
and the three written by Avelino Rodrigues, and associates,
draw heavily on Otelo's orientation.

What is suggested by this brief review is that we are very
much in need of a book which brings together the many
strands of the Portuguese revolution and analyzes them in the

light of historical and then post-revolutionary developments. Such is the purpose of this book. In light of the critical comments above, my effort must be everything the above works were not. Because of the high level of journalistic and even academic misinformation, the complexity of the case, and the ongoing dynamic, this is not an easy task. This is particularly so for the experience in Portugal brings up the most fundamental questions in political science: namely, the causes of revolution, the formation of regimes, and the interaction of domestic and international factors in specific political contexts. To aim for less is inappropriate, yet it is essential that one take into consideration the interaction of many variables that are difficult to separate, let alone analyze. This case study, then, is an effort to analyze the formation of the new regime in Portugal by giving specific attention to and attempting to integrate a very wide spectrum of variables.

As my intention here is to analyze rather than describe, the question immediately arises as to which approach or framework will be employed. I do not intend to formulate a new and complete framework for the analysis of all possible cases of regime-formation and thus do not feel compelled to review all earlier frameworks.[2] What seems most appropriate is a perspective in which Portugal is seen as passing through a rapid process of modernization after decades and maybe even centuries of stagnation. From the height of power in the fifteenth century, Portugal sunk to the lowest levels of socioeconomic indicators in the 1960s, was ruled by a conservative authoritarian regime, and sought to retain colonies while other more modern countries surrendered theirs. In many respects the revolution of 1974 can be viewed as an attempt to catch up with the rest of the world, and the instability in politics a reflection of the many contradictory strategies put forth to bring about some form of modernization. The present proposed entry into the EEC is clearly an attempt to link Portugal more closely to the Western European pattern of modernization. Modernization, then, is the overall perspective that will be utilized in this analysis of Portuguese politics since 1974. I define modernization as the process whereby countries come to resemble others already further along a social, political, and economic path initiated with the Industrial and the French Revolutions. Involved is industrialization or the increasing application of inanimate sources of energy, and increases in such processes as secularization, participation, education, and communication. There are, of course, a number of competing views on the utility of some form of modernization perspective, and while I am aware of these criticisms I still feel that it is appropriate in this case.[3] The general perspective need not imply that being modern is necessarily good, that there are pure polar positions of tradition and modernity, that all countries will follow the same path toward modernization, or that there is a pure and unambiguous position of modern that any country has achieved. Rather, the perspective as I am employing it suggests that some countries have passed through an on-going process, whereby they industrialized and the society changed. Concurrently, the relationship between the rulers and the ruled has also altered, and the state has come to play a more dominant role in directing society.

In the case of Portugal the present process of modernization has occurred through the revolution of 1974. The general perspective utilized here for the relationship of state and society is suggested in the following quote from Reinhard Bendix: "In studies of the modernization of complex societies, it is more useful to consider social structure and government, or society and the state, as interdependent, but also relatively autonomous, spheres of thought and action."[4] In this orientation one analyzes the relationship of state and society and does not assume that the former is determined by the latter. The state, in short, can maintain a certain autonomy from the society. What is more, political elites can play a role through the exercise of power in determining the actions of the state. The general orientation, then, in this book is set at an intermediate or middle level and does not neglect governmental structures nor the role of political actors.[5]

My underlying assumptions are: that politics is conflict over scarce resources in which the institutions themselves are fought for and with, while necessarily remaining somewhat autonomous from society; that conflict is channeled through structures; that regimes can be analyzed according to which groups, and thus conflict, are included in or excluded from decision making; and that elites do, in fact, have a role in superseding conflicts and thus formulating stable regimes. The main themes to be pursued thus concern the nature of the structures and organizations, the conflicts, and the solutions that elites devise for ruling. This general orientation is nicely elaborated by Adam Przeworski in the following summary regarding the transition to democracy:

First, democracy is a form of institutionalization of contin-
ual conflicts. Secondly, the capacity of particular groups to
realize their interests is shaped by the specific institutional
arrangements of a given system. Finally, although this capacity is given a priori, outcomes of conflicts are not
uniquely determined either by the institutional arrangements or by places occupied by participants within the system of production.

And, "The process of establishing democracy is a process of institutionalizing uncertainty, or subjecting all interests to uncertainty."[6] The main problem, then, is how to institutionalize
uncertainty, as "The solutions to the democratic compromise
consist of institutions." Of course democratic patterns are
only a small part of all possible patterns and have been limited
in their application both historically and geographically.

Juan J. Linz remains the most prolific and persuasive proponent of this general approach which I am discussing here
and writes in detail on a somewhat similar case, that of Spain.
There is, however, one constraint to his approach which becomes obvious when analyzing Portugal, and this concerns
the role of international variables in regime-formation and collapse.[7] Linz does not deal with this element in any detail in
his analysis, yet its importance in the present case will be obvious.

In most of the literature dealing with the general orientation I find useful, the focus has been on authoritarianism, military rule, and the demise or breakdown of democracy.[8] In this
case, however, the establishment of a liberal democratic regime has left social scientists not particularly well prepared by
the specifics of this literature, although there is now concern
with analyzing the establishment or reestablishment of democratic formats.[9] The traditional literature on democratic systems tends to be country-specific and is by and large static in
dealing with comparisons. Probably most useful are the insights of the Weberians such as Reinhard Bendix and Randall
Collins who look to the emergence of competing groups or
classes vis-à-vis the state rather than to some putative cultural heritage.[10] Of course, group formation is related to levels
of modernization and thus we must pay attention to what is
possible at any particular level.

In light of the above, it is clear that in order to analyze the
formation of the Portuguese regime since 1974 we must look
to the nature of the institutions composing or defining it, see

what type of link there is with the population and the attitudes of sectors of this population, and the type and degree of involvement of foreign actors (widely defined). And, all of this must be seen in terms of conflicts and tensions between groups and institutions.

Chapter One will describe the low level of modernization in Portugal and discuss the "Estado Novo" that perpetuated this situation in the twentieth century. Chapter Two will analyze the collapse of this regime and describe how the coup led to a revolution; some of the most important changes will be discussed in Chapter Three. The next chapter deals with the manner in which the revolution was limited and how the regime began by evolving into a liberal democratic pattern. In Chapter Five the experiences of the governments after the Constitution of 1976 will be described and the structures of government defined. The question is then raised of the continuity of the changes brought about in the revolution, and in Chapter Six the results of a public opinion poll indicating the degree of support for these changes are discussed. In Chapter Seven the international supports and constraints on this same process are outlined and summarized and constitutional revision discussed. The Conclusion will attempt to integrate some of the findings from the chapters in order to appreciate what path(s) to modernization is likely for Portugal today.

Notes: Introduction

1. For an excellent review of much of this literature in German see Guy Clausse, "A mais recente literatura de expressão alemã sobre problemas económicos e sociais em Portugal: Uma visão crítica," *Estudos de Economia* 3 (October-December, 1982) 91–96.

2. An excellent review of the most appropriate frameworks and the formulation of another may be found in Part One of Alfred Stepan, *The State and Society: Peru in Comparative Perspective* (Princeton: Princeton University Press, 1978).

3. One critique which finds little to recommend a modernization approach is Dean Tipps, "Modernization Theory and the Comparative Study of Societies: A Critical Perspective," *Comparative Studies in Society and History* 15 (1978): 199–226. Another critique which finds utility in the general approach is Reinhard Bendix, "Tradition and Modernity Reconsidered," *Comparative Studies in Society and History* 9 (1967): 292–346. An extremely useful review of some approaches to modernization and then an application is Elbaki Hermassi, *The Third World Reassessed* (Berkeley: University of Califor-

nia Press, 1980), pp. 16–40. My general perspective has been defined by reliance on a general Weberian approach to analysis. However, it has also been influenced by the work of such scholars as Peter Evans, Barrington Moore, Jr., and Theda Skocpol. See, for example, Peter Evans, *Dependent Development* (Princeton: Princeton University Press, 1979); Barrington Moore, Jr., *Social Origins of Dictatorship and Democracy: Lord and Peasant in the Making of the Modern World* (Boston: Beacon Press, 1967); and Theda Skocpol, *States and Social Revolutions* (Cambridge: Cambridge University Press, 1979).

4. Bendix, "Tradition and Modernity Reconsidered," p. 333.

5. The level which I wish to suggest is that dealt with in the works of scholars such as Ralf Dahrendorf and Juan Linz. See, for example, Ralf Dahrendorf, "Conflict and Liberty: Some Remarks on the Social Structure of German Politics," *British Journal of Sociology* 14 (1963): 197–211 and *Class and Class Conflict in Industrial Society* (Stanford: Stanford University Press, 1959). Juan J. Linz, *The Breakdown of Democratic Regimes: Crisis, Breakdown, and Reequilibration* (Baltimore: Johns Hopkins University Press, 1978). Also very stimulating is Charles Tilly, "Does Modernization Breed Revolution?," *Comparative Politics* 5 (April 1973): 425–47.

6. Adam Przeworski, "Some Problems in the Study of the Transition to Democracy," Working Paper Number 61 Latin American Program, The Wilson Center, Smithsonian Institution, (1979) pp. 13–14.

7. A very useful review of the literature on regimes and international variables is Peter Gourevitch, "The Second Image Reversed: The International Sources of Domestic Politics," *International Organization* 32 (1978): 881–911.

8. Linz, *The Breakdown of Democratic Regimes*, is an extremely concise exposition of a very useful approach to the topic. For a good selection of essays dealing with a particular approach to this topic (the "Bureaucratic-Authoritarian" model) see David Collier, ed., *The New Authoritarianism in Latin America* (Princeton: Princeton University Press, 1979).

9. The Latin American Program of the Wilson Center, Smithsonian Institution, held seminars on this topic. It should be noted that international variables are largely ignored in these analyses. See for example, Kevin Middlebrook, "Prospects for Democracy: Regime Transformation and Transitions from Authoritarian Rule: A Rapporteur's Report," Working Paper Number 62 (1979). The Working Papers are available from the Program.

10. Randall Collins, "A Comparative Approach to Political Sociology," in *State and Society,* ed. Reinhard Bendix. (Boston: Little, Brown, 1968), pp. 42–67. On Reinhard Bendix's work see, in particular, *Nation-Building and Citizenship: Studies of our Changing Social Order* (New York: John Wiley & Sons, 1964), and his "Tradition and Modernity Reconsidered."

1

The Economic and Political Background to Current Portuguese Modernization

The roots of the crisis in state and society which led to the coup of April 25, 1974, and then to revolution can be found in the lack of modernization which became manifest in the nineteenth century. Portugal did not experience an Industrial Revolution, with all the implications this held for social and political structures in other parts of Europe, but retained instead more traditional patterns in all realms of economy, society, and state. What is more, the regime established in the third decade of the twentieth century sought to maintain these traditional patterns. In this chapter I will discuss the background to the lack of modernization and show how the regime of Premier Oliveira Salazar sought to perpetuate it by means of a political system which did not permit conflict or the representation of interests.

The type of political system established in Portugal from at least the sixteenth century is most appropriately termed patrimonial.[1] It was a system characterized by a strong central political authority, which did not rely on nobles for the implementation of policy. This was possible because in the reconquest of both Spain and Portugal from the Moors, power was centralized in a single apparatus utilizing a military force primarily loyal to this apparatus. From the period of discoveries, then, the tradition was established of a centralized power which was hegemonic in the small and cohesive territory of Portugal (and less so in the colonies), which controlled not only the military but also the Catholic Church.[2] The Counter Reformation had its basis in the Iberian Peninsula which served to further consolidate the control over the

Church so that the patrimonial system was little threatened by Protestant sects and churches which promoted pluralism in other parts of Europe. Thus from the fifteenth century there was little challenge to the strong central power of the Crown.

One must query how this type of system survived while other absolutisms decayed and democratic and industrial revolutions changed the nature of society and politics. Indeed, I am not suggesting that no political change occurred, but rather that the general pattern of Portuguese centralized authority continued despite episodic political changes.[3] In addition to the initial centralized political structure, we must consider Portugal's integration into world patterns of trade at the time of Britain's emergence as an economic power. Portugal was, in the words of António de Figueiredo "no more than a satellite of the British super-power."[4] The relationship of dependence between Portugal and Britain is symbolized by a series of commercial treaties dated 1642, 1654, 1661, and 1703 (Methuen Treaty). As Sideri has stated, "The Anglo-Portuguese relationship which emerged from this economic arrangement was one of strong dependence by Portugal on England, although it reinforced the Braganza House and the landed interests, and thus the aristocracy and the church."[5] The scholarship on this question concludes that the type of commercial relationship entered into, at least initially without use of coercion on the part of the British, was to keep the level of industrialization in Portugal minimal as the country became defined as an exporter of primary and raw goods. The implications for manufacturing and the expansion of industrialization in what have been called the "core countries" has been studied as have the results of those which did not industrialize. This is what the literature on "the world system" and dependency deals with.[6] Portugal's economy remained backward, primary, and weak. The studies have shown that whereas Britain ran surpluses Portugal ran deficits, and thus the lessons of both Ricardo and particularly Adam Smith on comparative advantages being beneficial to both partners must be reconsidered.[7] Portugal stagnated despite the colonial market and was unable to take advantage of the possibilities of manufacturing.

In Portugal the continuity from the patrimonial system and the situation of dependence can also be explained in part by the possession of a colonial empire. Despite the ongoing trade deficits and the lack of industrialization, Portugal could

survive with its patrimonial system and its class structure intact because of the tremendous influx of colonial goods including raw materials, gems, and bullion. Thus while the economic
structures of Portugal itself were extremely weak, the importation of goods from the colonies hid the fundamental
weaknesses of these structures.[8] From its colonial reliance as
early as the sixteenth century, we can begin to appreciate the
mentality which would seek to perpetuate a colonial empire in
Africa even until the late twentieth century. The importation
of goods allowed for the continuation of the centralized political system and the perpetuation of the traditional class structure, which meant that the country was neither interested in
nor obliged to adopt technological and social innovations from
the period of the seventeenth to twentieth centuries. In short,
Portugal remained unmodern while other countries modernized and grew stronger. Such a situation was self-perpetuat-
ing: the longer society resisted change the more difficult it
became to break out of its entrenched position, particularly
given the interaction of domestic elites and international links
and constraints.

Reformist political movements sprang up in the late nineteenth century, but as Sideri has shown they did not succeed
because of a lack of economic resources. This was due to the
loss of Brazil in the third decade of the century and to a general
retreat from external commercial activity in the face of British
expansion throughout the world.[9] Again we see that the internal situation is indeed linked to external constraints and once
established is perpetuated. We might observe as well that the
colonies in Africa were almost lost to the British in the late
nineteenth century when Britain and Germany negotiated for
the division of southern Africa.

It would take us too far afield to cover the political history
of the late nineteenth century. Our purpose here is to but provide the rudiments of Portuguese economic and political history in order to understand the causes of the coup of April 25,
1974, and the subsequent need for modernization. We must,
however, pay a certain amount of attention to the Republic of
1910–1926, for it was the failure of this republic which led to
the founding of the regime of Premier Oliveira Salazar which
restored and perpetuated the patrimonial pattern of state and
society for nearly half a century.

There are a number of more specific reasons for reviewing
the Republic. First, this was the initial attempt in Portugal to

establish a democratic republic and as democracy normally implies a certain degree of mobilization, one might anticipate that through it some amount of modernization would have been achieved. Second, the particularly unhappy experience of the Republic was used by Oliveira Salazar to justify many aspects of the Estado Novo and we can better understand the latter by seeing it in contrast to the former. Finally, after 1974 many Portuguese and foreigners have tried to equate the instability of the present political system to that suffered by the Republic of 1910–1926. We can better appreciate this comparison by briefly reviewing the earlier period which was, in my view, extremely different from the present.

The Republic was unique vis-à-vis the regimes which preceded it. As Wheeler states, "In my view, the First Republic, despite some structural connections with nineteenth century liberalism, was a complex, singular phenomenon which attempted, despite its failure, to put into practice its ideals and which like no regime before it, was forced to pay the cost, both human and non-human."[10] Despite this new form of regime, the society in which it was founded was extremely unmodern. The population was 80 percent rural, and of the remaining 20 percent over half lived in the two cities of Lisbon and Porto. More than 60 percent of the population were in agriculture and less than 20 percent in secondary industries—and of these many were in crafts. Out of a population of 6 million, there were a maximum of 100,000 persons who might be called proletarians, and except for a small elite of aristocrats and middle class, the rest of the population was peasantry. In 1911 some 70 percent of the population was illiterate. Clearly, then, the society was not modern, yet the Republic was a political system based on the more modern countries of northern Europe.[11]

Throughout the Republic there was one party, the Democrats, which usually held power in the Congress and in the administration. This party, like most of the others, was an amalgam of factions, and while there was some effort to bring about change in the society the greatest amount of political energy was used for internal political battles. The results are easily recognized in the extreme political instability. The sixteen years of the Republic have been characterized by Wheeler in terms of "an ongoing political crisis, an interrupted civil war, and a latent state of siege." Portugal's Republic was the most unstable government in Europe, and during the 16 years there were nine presidents, 44 governments, 25 uprisings, and three counter-revolutionary dictatorships. Juan Linz has prepared a table on cabinet instability in European parliamentary systems between World War I and II. At the head of the list, before Yugoslavia, Spain, and Germany is Portugal with an average government duration of 117 days.[12] The Republic, being founded in an extremely backward society which was heavily dependent on the rest of Europe, found the elites competing and bickering among themselves rather than seeking to modernize the society. It was, by all accounts, a failure as a political system and provided real justification for the regime which followed it, as the Estado Novo based its legitimacy for order and stability on the disorder and instability of the Republic. Additionally, this regime prided itself on maintaining the traditional system of society which would not give rise to conflicts, as it favorably contrasted itself to the Republic and other liberal and democratic systems. What is more, it would look back to a glorified Portuguese past: the Republic aspired to bring Portugal at least up to the nineteenth century; the "Estado Novo" would leap back to the fifteenth. As society was indeed backward enough there was some basis to this tactic, and ample possibilities existed for the formation and maintenance of a predemocratic regime.

A number of terms have been employed to characterize the regime formulated and supervised by Premier Antonio de Oliveira Salazar from 1928 until his incapacitating stroke in 1968. "Fascist" has been used frequently, but this is misleading for the regime lacked a mobilizing mass party characteristic of Italian and German fascism, nor did it promote an ideology of extreme nationalism and expansionism. There is good material elaborating the dissimilarities of Salazarism and fascism and I will not dwell on the point here.[13] The more appropriate terms are "clerical-conservative" and "corporatist-authoritarian." We must remember that Salazar came into power not at the head of a movement but rather as an individual—albeit linked with others through the CADC (Academic Centre for Christian Democracy). This is not to suggest that he was clerical for although he studied in the seminary and maintained close links with the Church and clerics, he was to rule in such a way that the Church too was kept in a subservient position.[14] In certain respects the regime was indeed corporatist; and for that matter, it was officially declared to be corporatist. However, ample studies now show that interest representation through corporatist structures failed to function and indeed the corporations themselves were formed only in 1956, some 33 years after the Estado Novo was officially founded.[15]

The most accurate term for conveying the sense of what the Salazar regime was and how it operated is "a conservative and authoritarian regime of personal rulership." It was conservative in ideology, or legitimation, and the structure of control. The legitimation was a combination of some elements of Catholicism along with bits and pieces of a glorified Portuguese past. Catholicism provided symbolism and the emphasis on authority: specific reference was made to Pope Leo XIII's "Rerum Novarum" which presumably supported the nonconflictual, nonantagonistic system of interest representation. The Portuguese past supplied the contribution to civilization, the discoveries, and indeed the ongoing parameters of the nation state, the oldest in Europe. The legitimation assumed different colorations, depending on events and trends outside Portugal, and could be termed fascist at all only because it was formed when this ideology was on the rise in Europe. The structure of control was also conservative in that it did not provide for change. As Graham has stated, "for all practical purposes, the making and implementation of public policy in the New State came to be limited to the bureaucratic arena." He notes further, "Control was established through the use of personalism, and Salazar utilized reciprocal relations effectively as a means for tying to himself those within his immediate constituency."[16] The structure of control was the bureaucracy and the repressive apparatus. Because Salazar formed it and guided it for all but the last six years of its existence, this regime was clearly a system of personal rulership. He designed it, made it function, and when it was passed on to Marcelo Caetano it did not work as it had for Salazar.[17]

The regime was authoritarian in that it denied structured access, and thus the representation of interests and conflicts, of most of the population. Corporatism did not represent these interests nor did the electoral system. There was but one official party or movement (the União Nacional), suffrage was so restricted as to be static even with population growth, the President was indirectly elected after 1959, and the National Assembly did not function as a policy-making body in this system. In short, participation and representation were severely limited, and the population did not participate in the decision-making system which was dominated by Salazar. Pluralism and mobilization were discouraged through anticipation, cooptation, and finally repression. The system was strongly controlled and whatever interests emerged in society had to be explicitly recognized by the central level rather than receiving procedural recognition.

With his long tenure in command and the force of personal control, Salazar implemented those ideas of a glorified rural past and the commitment to balanced budgets which gave a particular coloration to the whole society. Antonio de Figueiredo characterizes Salazar's rulership in terms of one running a small rural estate and José António Saraiva puts it in similar terms: "Salazar administered the State as a small businessman of the province administers his business."[18] In this regime the social and economic stability, and thus backwardness, were prized to the detriment of other values and the country by and large stagnated.

It would be difficult to argue that Salazar was controlled by any particular class. That the aristocracy, the rural elite, the commercial, and finally an industrial elite benefited from his rule is obvious. However, it would be inaccurate to state that any group controlled him for in the pattern of patrimonial rule, updated in this conservative and authoritarian regime of personal control, Salazar alone ruled. He was, as Cabral argues, autonomous from all groups, and thus with minimal obligations to them.[19] Or, as Pinto states it, "He came directly from the University to Power. This is extremely important in the sense of his independence and authority for he was free of clienteles and compromises which in the modern world one must pay attention to. He received power on his own conditions without having to fight for it."[20]

The regime he created was endowed with a full set of charters, institutions, norms, and regulations much in line with his strictly orthodox economic and legalistic training. All was regulated and everything found its precise location and specification according to how Salazar wished it to be done. This indeed made for order and stability and little innovation. Salazar intentionally isolated Portugal from the outside world for he feared its corrosive influences on the country. Not only was censorship severe, the secret police pervasive, but Portugal, despite the fact of being a charter member of NATO, minimized the amount of Marshall Plan aid it would accept. And this in an extremely poor country.[21] The amount of foreign investment was also restricted, as was indeed the level of industrialization permitted. In short, the country was intentionally kept apart from the modern world and a strong regime established which intentionally disregarded the possible wishes of the population. Salazar sought isolation and designed a government which was largely autonomous from society in that it did not have to rely on any particular class to stay in power. It was a brilliant example of institutional design which rested only on him. ~

Despite the low level of Portugal's modernization and the enforced passivity of the population, some change and innovation was essential to prevent the regime from becoming anachronistic. During Salazar's rule such change was not allowed, and if anything the regime became more rigid in the face of the outbreak of guerrilla warfare in Angola in 1961. But what did change were the regulations concerning foreign investment which were modified to encourage investment in Portugal and the colonies. This was but part of Portugal's slight opening up to the outside world, built on the joining of the EFTA in 1959 and membership in GATT, and to be followed up in an intended agreement with the EEC after 1970. Thus, pragmatic reasons dictated a shift in one of Salazar's key tenets: a minimization of foreign investment in Portugal. Part of this shift involved the revision of the restrictions on industrialization (through Condicionamento Industrial) which were substantially modified in 1965. Thus the economy was changing, transactions increasing with the outside world, and foreign loans negotiated.[22]

The opportunity for political change presented itself in 1968 when a stroke incapacitated Salazar from governing. He died two years later. Marcelo Caetano was selected as his replacement and had made something of a name for himself, first as an understudy of Salazar and then entering into a certain degree of opposition over the question of university autonomy. At the time of his selection he promised an opening, a certain liberalization, which seemed appropriate given the changes then taking place in the economy and society. There was talk of reforms pertaining to the colonies, the election of a group of Liberals or progressives in the elections of 1969 to the National Assembly, the name of the political movement was changed to National Popular Action (ANP), and the name of the secret police to General Directorate of Security (DGS).

These suggestions were of a rather far-reaching nature in a regime which was now free of the control of its founder and leader for some forty years.

By 1973, however, it was clear that the change or reform was aborted, the government was firmly entrenched, and in fact repression was on the increase precisely because there was so little change. The incumbent president, Admiral Américo Tomás, despite the fact that he was 78 years of age, succeeded himself in the indirect election of July 25, 1972. The progressives in the National Assembly had resigned by 1973 because they realized the futility of their position in this body with minimal powers of decision making. The elections to the National Assembly in 1973 were even more formalistic than usual, the opposition did not participate, and the key issue, that of the status of the colonies in Africa, was not allowed on the agenda. In short, the regime was increasingly intransigent and refused to innovate.

It is quite clear that Caetano lacked control of the regime. If he did not rule, and he presumably had more power than the president, it meant that inertia ruled; in fact, the system formulated by Salazar merely kept moving on its own, even if quite slowly. The sense of this is captured well in the following quote from José António Saraiva:

> Caetano received from Salazar the immense, uncontrollable, and unmovable weight of an extremely centralized bureaucratic machine, [which was] meticulously adjusted, perfected, and tested during 36 years by only one person—a machine superseded by history but which found its unmeasurable inertia in its capacity to passively resist any wish to change, the real reason of its force.[23]

Caetano, himself, in his book *Depoimento* constantly laments his lack of power and control. He bemoans the absence of a political party to back him, the uncooperative attitude of the Liberals, the inactivity and passivity of the country's capitalists, and complains that his decisions do not become laws. It is a sad and tragic statement of powerlessness and the lack of political will. Thus despite Caetano's efforts at experimentation and change, the system remained by and large the same.[24] Graham summarizes the situation well. "While the regime remained no less authoritarian, Caetano was never successful in concentrating in his own hands the great influence and prestige which Salazar possessed during most of his lifetime. As a bureaucrat nurtured by the system, Caetano was to a considerable extent its prisoner."[25]

What is even more tragic was the fact that this same system which captured and ensnarled Caetano did the same with the population and the few groups or organizations which supposedly represented them. The population itself was controlled through the structures of the corporatist and authoritarian state which allowed no lower level of government control over any higher level. Through the corporatist systems, including gremios and casas do povo, as well as the structure of municipal government, the population was not allowed representation, let alone control. Political activity was conceded only at the time of elections and then under extremely severe control. Parties, with the exception of the clandestine PCP, did not develop, and the opposition politicians (or would-be party politicians) had very slight roles in the regime. Reading the statements by Caetano and comparing them to those of Mario Soares before 1974 gives one the sense of the lack of options on all sides; Caetano realized he did not have power whereas Soares knew he did not, thought that Caetano did, and could conceive of no ready way to obtain this supposed power.[26] He and others in the opposition, including the PCP, were resigned to their impotence and lacked plans for taking power. As noted above, the Liberals withdrew from the National Assembly. Reformist associations such as SEDES emerged to question and criticize the regime, but they too played little actual role in the system. In sum, if there was any power it was in the structures of the system and not, after the death of Salazar, in the hands of an individual or even a group. In the absence of any viable alternative the opposition was occupied by exiles abroad who would speak and criticize, but with little impact within Portugal itself as the regime became increasingly closed and defensive by 1973.

Undoubtedly the main cause for the inflexibility and intransigence of the regime, and the cause of its eventual downfall, was the ongoing colonial empire in Africa. The fact of empire was cemented in the whole historical definition of Portugal as an independent country. So miniscule in itself, and so vulnerable to invasion from the French and Spanish, the country in the twentieth century was economically vulnerable to all countries more modern than itself. As these facts became more widely recognized, Portugal, particularly under Salazar, would find its definition increasingly in its "colonial vocation." This empire, which was the third largest in the world in the era of colonial empires, was some 22 times the size of Portugal itself and the common statement was that "without the empire Portugal would be a small country." The heritage of discoveries, the civilizing mission, and a colonial vocation would continue, and this mystique was explicitly utilized by Salazar and then Caetano. In short, the presence of an empire was central to the definition of Portugal as an independent nation.[27]

It is illustrative of Salazar's priorities that he decreed the Colonial Act before the Constitution of the Estado Novo (1930 and 1933 respectively). According to Salazar, the colonial empire was both integral to the definition of Portugal as a nation and was necessary for the economic health of the country.[28] He was adamant in refusing to tolerate any question of decolonization, despite the wave of decolonization after World War II when larger and more powerful European countries were forced to grant independence. Even the example of the French being forced from Algeria was not enough; at approximately this time (1961) he would allow no negotiation with India over the Portuguese enclaves, and it was then as well that the fighting began in Angola which would later spread to Mozambique and Guinea. Even into the 1970s Portugal was seriously seeking to consolidate a centralized bureaucratic empire in which Lisbon would predominate over larger and richer Angola which was by then in a process of rapid development.

There is much to be said on the question of the economic benefits and liabilities of Portuguese colonialism. Unfortunately there is still no definitive study on this extremely important and complex topic. Substantial benefits derived by Portugal from the colonies include the following: exportation to the colonies of noncompetitive manufactured goods as well as low quality wine; importation of primary goods such as petroleum and coffee at advantageous prices; direct payment to Portugal by South Africa of gold bullion for Mozambiquian workers; sale to South Africa of colonial products which would include electricity with the completion of the huge Cabora Bassa dam. The colonies were not allowed to become financial burdens on Portugal, for the budgeting system forced them to pay their own way. Thus, in general terms, Portugal gained from the maintenance of a colonial empire. Money was brought in and supplies of raw materials guaranteed.[29] Obviously, some groups benefited more than others, and the nation as a whole probably lost in the long run: resources which might have gone to the ultimate development of Portugal were diverted to the waging of the wars. Additionally, the strain in human and moral terms of this colonialism/wars was extremely severe, and Portugal became something of an international pariah with very few friends indeed.

The combination of these economic, historical, and even psychological reasons, in conjunction with the nature of the conservative-authoritarian regime, created a very difficult situation in which to change policies. Caetano in his *Depoimento* makes it clear that from the beginning of his tenure the most important consideration, or preoccupation, was Africa.[30] The catch-22 situation was that Portugal was too small and weak to do without these colonies. It, unlike France or the United States, could not compete internationally and maintain a neocolonial system. Once independent (and in fact even before independence) the colonies could trade internationally and Portugal would suffer economically.[31]

Given the underlying economic reasons, but in which historical and psychological factors played an important part if only in allowing the regime to enjoy some degree of passive support from the population, the country maintained its political and military commitment to retain the colonial empire. The stakes were very large indeed for the granting of independence to the colonies would mean the end of an historical era, the loss of legitimacy of a regime which had defined itself through the colonial vocation, and obvious economic losses. But, retention of the colonies was costly. The Portuguese would find themselves fighting on three fronts, against guerrillas increasingly better armed and supported abroad, and against the tides of decolonization which appeared overwhelming. Portugal thus underwent a mass mobilization which brought the country second only to Israel in terms of the population under arms to total population.[32] Yet this mass mobilization occurred in a country in which emigration had been one of the defining characteristics since long before the outbreak of the wars. Portugal was, in short, a country unable to provide sufficient employment in industry for its population, but one which called up mass levies of men to maintain a system which kept the country underdeveloped. This contradiction would remain unresolved for several years due to the reasons noted above concerning the lack of structures of representation for the masses of the population. The more operative contradiction would be that concerning the development of Portugal by means of foreign investment and increasing integration in different patterns of trade.

With the change in laws in 1965, foreign investment as a percentage of Portuguese industry increased from 1.5 in 1960 to 27 in 1970.[33] This increase was imperative: to fight the wars and to remove some of the grievances in the colonies concerning domination from Lisbon, the country (including the colonies) had to be opened up. This opening up would hold implications for social change with an increasing number of industrial workers (something Salazar had feared) and an increased potential for the formation of unions. What is more, it would of necessity link Portugal more closely to international patterns of trade and thus render it increasingly vulnerable to fluctuations, particularly when the country was so underdeveloped and had a small domestic economy. These fluctuations would contravene the basis of the system created by Salazar which was order and stability: its sound currency, substantial reserves of foreign exchange and gold, and its extremely low inflation.[34] Further, with development, investment, and greater linking, the trade patterns of Portugal moved away from the colonies and toward OECD countries—particularly those in the enlarged EEC. Thus while it was clear that certain groups would continue to benefit from the colonial empire, it became less justified in an economic sense as trade was reoriented and as foreign investors became directly involved in the colonies.[35] There might be some serious question, then, of the value of retaining the colonies particularly in light of the costs in loss of life, disruption of families, loss of resources, and international ostracism, if the country's trade was simultaneously decreasing with these colonies.

This fundamental issue was posed in Portuguese politics, at least the bureaucratic politics which passed as politics in Portugal, in the early 1970s over the question of the "Europeanists." When Caetano took office, he brought in a group of technocrats who would presumably assist in reorienting the economy in a rational way toward Europe. However, politically this group, and in a sense Caetano himself, lost out against the Africanist faction; a situation which became manifest in the Cabinet reshuffle of July 1972. Those winning this internal battle held that Portugal's survival depended on an ongoing presence in Africa, even though this demanded the tremendous commitment of men and resources. Thus, despite the reorientation of trade, there was no parallel reorientation of politics to deal with the changed situation. The regime was too archaic, too disconnected, and inflexible to be able to respond to changes in the environment.

It is clear from testimonies as well as scholarly studies that Portuguese industry was under the control of the state and not competitive.[36] Decisions made in the state, then, were that much more important; apparently those influencing policy represented the noncompetitive and colonial groups. The competitive entrepreneurs and politicians were already involved with foreign investment, both in Portugal and externally. The tradition in Portugal was in terms of "condicionamento industrial" which controlled patterns of industrialization and led to the formation of a limited number of noncompetitive monopolies and trusts which expanded into broad areas of the economy. As this economic sector was also part and parcel of the regime, it merely highlights once again the tied-up or rigid nature of the system.

In 1973, with the wars raging in Africa and Guinea-Bissau declaring its independence, Portugal was hard hit by oil price increases, an Arab oil boycott, the general recession, and its tentative but not well-rationalized involvement in world economic patterns. The impact was severe with the decrease in workers' remittances, a decreased demand for immigrant workers in Europe, a decline in tourism, and an imported inflation which judging from the early months of 1974 would be some 35 percent. The sociopolitical results of this situation, in which the political system or regime was intransigent, proved to be strikes, demonstrations, and general disenchantment with a corresponding increase in violence on the part of the security apparatus. It was a tense time in Portugal, and it was obvious that there was no political solution to the crisis of society nor to the colonial situation which was the cause of much of it. There would be no response at all from the regime which had shown itself incapable of innovating through the late Salazar's and subsequent Caetano's tenure in office. In short, the pattern of modernization had not proven out.[37]

Notes

1. On the patrimonial regime see in particular Magali Sarfatti, *Spanish Bureaucratic-Patrimonialism in America* (Berkeley: Insti-

tute of International Studies, 1965). For an analysis of this system in contrast to northern European systems see Stanley and Barbara Stein, *The Colonial Heritage of Latin America* (New York: Oxford University Press, 1970).

2. For some details, a general discussion, and citations on this topic see Chapter 1 of my *The Political Transformation of the Brazilian Catholic Church* (Cambridge: Cambridge University Press, 1974), pp. 11–25. For a great many details see P. Miguel de Oliveira, *História Eclesiástica de Portugal*, 4th ed. (Lisboa: União Gráfica, 1968).

3. This perspective is elaborated extremely well in the small monograph of Francisco Sarsfield Cabral, *Uma Perspectiva Sobre Portugal* (Lisbon: Moraes Editores, 1973).

4. Antonio de Figueiredo, *Portugal: Fifty Years of Dictatorship* (Middlesex: Penguin Books, 1975), p. 36.

5. S. Sideri, *Trade and Power: Informal Colonialism in Anglo-Portuguese Relations* (Rotterdam: Rotterdam University Press, 1970), p. 5. See also António Fonseca Ferreira, *A Acumulação Capitalista Em Portugal* (Porto: Ediçoes Afrontamento, 1977), pp. 55–132, and H.E.S. Fisher, "Anglo-Portuguese Trade 1700–1770," in *The Growth of English Overseas Trade in the Seventeenth and Eighteenth Centuries*, ed. H.E. Minchinton (London: Methuen & Co., 1969).

6. A good review of this literature is Peter Gourevitch, "The Second Image Reversed: The International Sources of Domestic Politics," *International Organization* 32 (1978): 881–911. See also Fernando Henrique Cardoso and Enzo Faletto, *Dependency and Development in Latin America* (Berkeley: University of California Press, 1979) (translated by Marjory Mattingly Urquidi).

7. See in particular Sideri, *Trade and Power*, and Fisher, "Anglo-Portuguese Trade."

8. See Cabral, *Uma Perspectiva Sobre Portugal*, pp. 54, 79.

9. Sideri, *Trade and Power*, pp. 5–6.

10. Douglas L. Wheeler, *Republican Portugal: A Political History 1910–1926* (Madison: The University of Wisconsin Press, 1978), pp. 255–56.

11. As detailed throughout Wheeler, *Republican Portugal*. This particular perspective on the lack of modernity is stressed in A.H. de Oliveira Marques, *A Primeira Republica Portuguesa* (Lisbon: Livros Horizonte, 1970).

12. Juan J. Linz, *The Breakdown of Democratic Regimes: Crisis, Breakdown, and Reequilibration* (Baltimore: The Johns Hopkins University Press, 1978), pp. 111–12.

13. See, for example, H. Martins, "Portugal," in *European Fascism*, ed. S.J. Woolf (London: Weidenfeld and Nicolson, 1968), pp. 302–36 and Manuel de Lucena, "The Evolution of Portuguese Corporatism under Salazar and Caetano," in *Contemporary Portugal:*

The Revolution and its Antecedents, eds. Lawrence Graham and Harry M. Makler (Austin: University of Texas Press, 1979).

14. On the Church and the regime see my "Church and State in Portugal: Crises of Cross and Sword," *Journal of Church and State*, 18 (1976): 463–91.

15. On corporatism see in particular Howard Wiarda, "The Corporatist Tradition and the Corporative System in Portugal: Structures, Evolving Transcended, Persistent," pp. 89–122 and Joyce Firstenberg Riegelhaupt, "Peasants and Politics in Salazar's Portugal: The Corporate State and Village 'Nonpolitics'," in Graham and Makler, *Contemporary Portugal*, pp. 167–90 as well as abundant sources cited there by Wiarda, Schmitter, and de Lucena.

16. Lawrence Graham, *Portugal: The Decline and Collapse of an Authoritarian Order*, Comparative Politics Series, vol. 5 (Beverly Hills: Sage Publications, 1975), p. 19.

17. This particular focus is elaborated in José António Saraiva, *Do Estado Novo à Segunda República* (Amadora: Livraria Bertrand, 1974), pp. 93–119.

18. Ibid., p. 56, Figueiredo, *Portugal: Fifty Years of Dictatorship*, chap. 2.

19. Cabral, *Uma Perspectiva*, p. 56.

20. Jaime Nogueira Pinto, *Portugal: Os Anos do Fim*, vol. 1 (Lisbon: Sociedade de Publicações Economia & Finanças, LDA, 1976), p. 34.

21. On this see Luc Crollen, *Portugal, the U.S. and NATO* (Louvain: Leuven University Press, 1973), pp. 94–97. See also Mario Soares, *Portugal's Struggle for Liberty* (London: George Allen & Unwin, 1975), p. 71 (translated by Mary Gawsworth).

22. On this topic see for example Francisco Pereira de Moura, *Por Onde Vai a Economia Portuguesa?* 4th ed. (Lisbon: Seara Nova, 1974), and Eduardo de Sousa Ferreira, *Portuguese Colonialism from South Africa to Europe* (Freiburg: Aktion Dritte Welt, 1972).

23. Saraiva, *Do Estado Novo*, p. 84.

24. Nogueira Pinto, *Portugal: Os Anos do Fim*, vol. 1, is particularly good on this. See p. 217 for example. Marcelo Caetano, *Depoimento* (Rio de Janeiro: Distribuidora Record, 1974).

25. Graham, *Portugal: The Decline and Collapse*, p. 17.

26. Soares, *Portugal's Struggle*, p. 202, for example.

27. There is a huge literature on this topic and see, for example, the good description by Antonio de Figueiredo, *Portugal and Its Empire* (London: Victor Gollancz, 1961); for a superb study on the nature of the relationship between Portugal and the most important colony see Gerald Bender, *Angola under the Portuguese: The Myth and the Reality* (Berkeley: University of California Press, 1978).

28. For example, Crollen, *Portugal, the U.S. and NATO*, p. 21, cites this position of Salazar.

29. Sousa Ferreira, *Portuguese Colonialism*, pp. 23–27, and Keith Middlemas, *Cabora Bassa: Engineering and Politics in Southern Africa* (London: Weidenfeld and Nicolson, 1975), p. 238, provide some details on this very important topic.

30. Caetano, *Depoimento*, pp. 15 and 17.

31. Graham, *Portugal: The Decline and Collapse*, pp. 17 and 23, deals with this question as does Middlemas, *Cabora Bassa*, p. 245.

32. Portugal, with 11.2 percent of regular armed forces to men of military age compared to the highest in the world, Israel with 12.8 percent. This was triple the ratio of the U.K. and double that of the U.S. in 1974.

33. Figueiredo, *Portugal: Fifty Years of Dictatorship*, p. 228. See also Crollen, *Portugal, the U.S. and NATO*, pp. 108–9.

34. For some general background see, for example, Armando de Castro, et al., *Sobre o Capitalismo Português* (Coimbra: Atlântida Editora, 1974); Ramiro da Costa, *O Desenvolvimento do Capitalismo em Portugal* (Lisbon: Cadernos Peninsulares, 1975), and Eugénio Rosa, *A Economia Portuguese en Numeros* (Lisbon: Moraes Editores, 1975).

35. These data are discussed in Graham, *Portugal: The Decline and Collapse*, pp. 21–23, and Gerald Bender, "Portugal and Her Colonies Join the Twentieth Century: Causes and Initial Implications of the Military Coup," *Ufahamu* (Winter 1974):125–29.

36. See Caetano, *Depoimento*, pp. 119–20; Pinto, *Portugal: Os Anosido Fim*, vol. 1, and Klaus Esser, et al., *Portugal's Industrial Policy in Terms of Accession to the European Community* (Berlin: German Development Institute, 1980).

37. Portugal remained the most underdeveloped country of Western Europe as defined by most indicators. For instance, the per capita income was behind other less developed countries such as Ireland, Greece, and even Yugoslavia and ahead of only Turkey among the OECD countries. For a study of industrial underdevelopment see Esser, et al., *Portugal's Industrial Policy.* For personal experience dramatizing this underdevelopment see Figueiredo, *Portugal: Fifty Years of Dictatorship.* See Appendix I.

2

The Overthrow of the Estado Novo: The Coup and the Revolution

The Estado Novo did not allow for change from within its circumscribed system nor for political activity whereby opposition groups could pressure for change from without. Therefore, the armed forces were the only group sufficiently organized and autonomous enough to either maintain the regime or overthrow it in the face of increasing popular opposition which was manifest by mid-1973. The coup created by the Armed Forces Movement (MFA) on April 25, 1974, was the response of a small group of middle-level officers to this situation. The coup, however, led to a revolution, and as there are a number of unique features to this process it is necessary that we analyze it in some detail. In the first part of this chapter the background in politics and the military will be discussed. In the second part the dynamics whereby the coup unleashed a revolutionary process will be analyzed. And in the next chapter the extent of revolutionary change will be briefly described.

In 1926 the coup, which destroyed the First Republic and ushered in almost half a century of authoritarian rule under the Estado Novo, was begun largely by higher-level officers who sought to put an end to an extremely unstable political system with little popular support. Demonstrating little ability to govern themselves, and in the face of a serious economic situation, they turned over power to Oliveira Salazar in 1928 who remade the regime in his own image. In 1974 the coup, which put an end to his Estado Novo, was made by middle-level officers (captains and majors) who sought to terminate the forced stability of the regime which persisted despite internal changes, the implications arising from increased links abroad, and, mainly, the impossibility of winning wars against guerrilla movements in three colonies. In overthrowing the regime, however, they found that there was little in the old system on which to build a new one and indeed it quickly and nearly totally collapsed. While these officers were extremely capable in military matters, they were less so in politics and for that matter lacked a coherent plan for ruling. It is almost as if the officers were surprised by the rapidity and totality of their coup; it obviously had been planned in great detail whereas its aftermath had been given less consideration. In turning over power to General Spínola on April 25, they discovered that while they lacked a plan they most certainly did not agree with his. A process was initiated, then, which led to revolutionary changes far beyond what these officers had originally envisaged.

The key to the coup was the ongoing conflict in Africa. Without the wars and the tremendous social and personal pressures they created, it is likely that the anachronistic regime would have persisted and slowly, hesitatingly changed from within as the country became more involved with other European countries. That is, a pattern in some ways resembling Spain's might have been followed. However, on so pressing a matter as the wars the regime remained intransigent and there was no structured way whereby opposition could be registered. Thus, despite the fact that it was increasingly obvious that the wars could not be won militarily, the regime was unable to respond. Whereas France in Algeria, and more contemporaneously the United States in Southeast Asia, were also involved in guerrilla wars, they were able to find political solutions—albeit extremely difficult solutions but ones which necessitated a change of government rather than the overthrow of a regime. The Portuguese regime, however, found its strength in inflexibility and intransigence, and thus resulted an all or nothing predicament: change the regime.

The gravity of the guerrilla wars for the Portuguese can be demonstrated in a number of ways. The defeat of the United States at roughly the same time was suggestive, particularly in light of the vast disparity in the military might of the U.S. and Portugal. The use made by the guerrillas (PAIGC) in Guinea-Bissau of ground-to-surface missiles for the first time in 1973 not only denied airspace to the Portuguese Air Force, but showed that the guerrillas now had access to armaments of equal or greater sophistication than those of the Portuguese. This realization had particularly important psychological effects on the military in Guinea-Bissau.[1] Furthermore, by this time some 50 countries already recognized the self-declared independence of Guinea-Bissau which suggested that the Portuguese presence there, militarily as well as diplomatically, was increasingly artificial and finite. Yet the regime of Marcelo Caetano insisted on holding on to not only Angola and Mozambique which were large, well-endowed with resources, and close to supportive Rhodesia and South Africa, but also to poor and isolated Guinea. The general consensus is that the wars were not yet lost to the Portuguese in Angola and Mozambique. Militarily the Portuguese could hold on for a few more years and maybe even longer if economic development occurred rapidly and the colonies were granted more autonomy.[2]

It was not only at the middle-level that officers realized all was not well. Indeed, at the highest level disenchantment with the management of the wars was evident as well. It is important to note, however, that the solutions advocated were contradictory. The strategy from the Right was to overthrow the regime of the "weak and vacillating Caetano" and pursue the wars more forcefully. This movement, headed by General Kaulza de Arriaga along with three other famous generals, became known in late 1973.[3] The solution was in the tradition of Rightist coups in which the highest levels in the military overthrow a regime, frequently founded by the military itself, in order to make it more rigorous and active. This coup attempt did not proceed because there was minimal support among the middle-level officers who had spent time in the field for continuing the wars and who realized the futility of continued fighting.

Rather they would support an orientation seeking a negotiated end to the wars. This strategy was most forcefully carried and defined by General Spínola. General Spínola served for five years as Military Governor of Guinea, and despite the innovative war he directed, realized that there would be no military solution for Portugal there. In 1972, and again in 1973, he attempted to convince Caetano of the impossibility of fighting the wars.[4] There is even some evidence that he proposed to Caetano that the two lead the country jointly and resolve the situation of the wars through political negotiation in some form of larger federation.[5] Caetano was unwilling, or more likely, unable to be flexible on the question of the colonies (indeed, it was a nonquestion or nonissue) and thus rejected the advice and suggestions of this prestigious man who had received the highest military honors and was famous both inside and outside of Portugal. Caetano's response to Spínola's suggestion for negotiation over Guinea-Bissau is symptomatic of his leadership and is suggestive of the stagnation of the regime in general:

> Even if negotiations over Guinea were successful, one could not forget that we held Angola and we held Mozambique, with hundreds of thousands of whites and millions of loyal blacks whom we could not sacrifice lightly. The difficulty of the problem of Guinea was this: it was part of a larger global problem that had to be considered and acted upon as a whole, while maintaining the legal and political principles which accompanied it. [thus he stated to General Spínola]
>
> For the overall defense of the Overseas [colonies] it is preferable to leave Guinea with an honourable military defeat rather than to negotiate with the terrorists, opening the door to other negotiations.
>
> But your Excellency would prefer a military defeat in Guinea, exclaimed the scandalized General.
>
> Armies are made to fight and must fight to win but it is not inevitable that they win. If the Portuguese Army is defeated in Guinea after having fought to the limit of its possibilities, this defeat would leave intact the legal-political possibilities of defending the rest of the Overseas. It is the duty of the government to defend all of the Overseas. . . .
>
> The General did not agree with the decision of the government—which represented not only my point of view, but all of those people I consulted (and they were many) without exception. And he returned to Bissau profoundly shocked and without hiding his anguish.[6]

Aware of the intransigency of Caetano's regime and realizing the gravity of the situation in the colonies, not only regarding the wars but also the disenchantment among the officers and men, Spínola decided to publish his book *Portugal and the Future*. The book appeared in February of 1974; its timely publication no less than the contents indicated to those who understood politics in Portugal that a solution would have to be found outside of the regime. This fact was even realized by Caetano as indicated in the following quote:

... on the 18th [February, 1974] I received a copy of the book *Portugal and the Future* with a friendly dedication of the author. I could not read it that day nor the following which was taken up by the Council of Ministers. Only on the 20th after a tiring day did I pick up the book after 11 at night. I did not stop reading before reaching the last page early in the morning. And when I closed the book I realized that the military coup d'état, which I had sensed for some months, was now inevitable.[7]

The publication of this book with such implications, despite rigorous censorship in Portugal, was in itself suggestive. Not unexpectedly, the regime's reaction was to remove Spínola and his superior, the Chief of Staff, General Costa Gomes, from their positions and to reaffirm the continued wars in the colonies. Sadly enough, even at this time the regime once again asserted its intransigence in this most important of all issues.

General Spínola had completed his tour in Africa and had been awarded four stars and a position especially created for him—Vice Chief of Staff. He may have published the book because of conclusions drawn from his tours of duty and in the expectation that his idea of a federation was possible. However, his interest in a high government position, probably the presidency which was normally occupied by a military man, was no secret, and he had apparently sought it in 1972 before Ameríco Tomás was again renewed in the office.[8] The publication of the book could have been expected to cause a shake-up in the regime at which point Spínola's friends in the military and among the large industrialists might have agitated sufficiently to oust Tomás and install Spínola as president. This was certainly possible. However, if this was his objective it did not succeed: the regime reasserted its traditional policy and closed in on itself. This reaction provided the catalyst for the MFA to initiate its coup. Thus, rather than a solution made at the highest levels there would be a shift within the military, the removal of the top levels of the regime and its military apparatus, and the opening for a revolution. Further, the relation between Spínola and the creators of the coup would define and determine political dynamics during the ensuing year.

It must be reemphasized that the coup of April 25 was not made by the upper echelon of the officer corps. Except for Generals Spínola and Costa Gomes there were no officers at the rank of general party to the coup. With very rare exceptions,

the higher officer corps were completely compromised by the
regime and unlikely to support an effort to overthrow it.
Wheeler has shown that senior officers not on active duty were
involved in any number of regime structures and functions,
from censorship to industry, and had little reason to be involved in political activity independent of the regime.[9] This
was not, then, a coup by the generals. Indeed, while Generals
Spínola and Costa Gomes knew of the preparations they were
not the leaders and in fact were included in the plans only at
the last moment. By the mere fact that this was a coup by the
middle ranks against the higher ranks already suggested that
it could bear radical implications.[10]

A conditioning factor to the coup was the class background of the middle-level officers. In the past, the officers had
been recruited from the upper and middle-middle classes and
were disposed to be "subjectively loyal" to the regime which
represented their interests. By the mid-1960s and the continuing African wars, as well as the diversification of opportuni-
ties in Portugal and abroad, there was less interest in joining
the officer corps. The class composition of the corps dropped to
provincial middle class and the urban lower-middle class; thus
the class interest of these men would presumably differ from
those of the higher class officer corps. There is evidence that
this difference was in fact perceived by the middle-level officers who noted that their superiors remained in Lisbon, collected relatively large stipends, lived well at the cost of the
nation, and were not exposed to danger.[11] A related element to
the changing class composition was the difficulty of finding
candidates for officer training. This difficulty was further evidence of the low popularity of the career, which was realisti-
cally viewed as uncomfortable, dangerous, and unsuccessful
in that the wars might well be lost. That is, the profession was
not what it could have been and increasingly it came to be perceived that the regime, through its intransigence and stupidity, was to blame for the ongoing wars and the reverses
suffered by the Portuguese armed forces in pursuing them.[12]

The process whereby the MFA was formed and perceived
the need for the coup is complex. Its beginning was in Guinea
which was the most difficult, or desperate, theater and where
General Spínola innovated in pursuing the war. Here he formulated a "minds and hearts" campaign which utilized some
elements of psychology and brought the officers into close con-
tact with the men and even with the PAIGC. In short, the senior

officer encouraged innovation, thought, and adaptation. It was in Guinea where the war was first lost due to geography and the sophisticated arms provided to the PAIGC. And, as previously discussed, Caetano would not budge and even tolerated the idea of a military defeat—if done with honor. The documents of the founders of the MFA, including Otelo Saraiva de Carvalho, Carlos Fabião, and Vasco Lourenço show clearly that they realized the war was already lost in Guinea.[13] Thus in purely professional, not to mention existential, terms there was substantial basis for resentment against the regime centered in Lisbon.

Despite Caetano's comment about a defeat with honor, the officers who would form the MFA had some indication of how they would be regarded if defeated. In 1961 Salazar had ordered the Portuguese military to fight the Indian Army despite overwhelming odds. When the Portuguese were defeated it was considered a national disgrace and the key officers were court-martialed. More recently, settlers in Mozambique had become outspoken in their criticism and had even stoned an officers' club (Beira in January 1974) when they felt that the armed forces were not providing adequate protection. Thus, the armed forces were being blamed. And back in Portugal in 1973, military and paramilitary groups promoted a Congress of Combattants in Porto which stressed that the fighting had to continue. Yet these were people who were not involved in the fighting, and there was an increasing sense among the officers in Africa that they would be the sacrificial lambs for the faults of the regime.[14]

During the height of the MFA radicalization in 1975 there appeared a certain amount of material in Portugal (much of it officially sponsored by the propaganda machine—the Fifth Division) and abroad on the MFA as a "liberation movement." The argument contends that the MFA read the texts of the guerrilla movements and even talked to the guerrillas themselves, became aware and radicalized, and decided to return and liberate Portugal. There is little basis to this view: the documents by and interviews with key elements do not support it; the strategy of forming a single party was not adopted; and the plan to "institutionalize" was both a fiasco and largely lacked legitimacy. This propaganda was a self-serving justification at a particular time to give the MFA a greater appeal and thus a larger role in controlling politics. The catalyst for the coup was not this liberation movement view, but rather a very concrete and real professional grievance which defined the middle-level officers against the regime and brought together a number of objective and subjective factors which finally led to action.

The middle-level officers, as noted above, were no longer from the upper classes and the military was their career. With the ongoing wars recruitment became difficult and there were not enough qualified candidates to fill the required positions. The regime, however, had to have officers and found a solution in an apparently rapid and efficient way. By means of Law #353 of July 1973, the government allowed individuals who had a certain amount of education and had already served in the armed forces to enter the officer corps after a course of six months. Upon fulfilling these conditions, they would be promoted to the same levels and receive the same benefits as those officers who had followed the full course at the military academy, for they were allowed to count the time they spent in the armed forces before being promoted. This was perceived as a direct threat to the prestige, integrity, and benefits of the officer corps as a professional status group, and served as the basis whereby the other factors came together and ultimately resulted in the coup. It provided the focus for meetings, letters, a broad exchange of ideas, and finally an awareness that the regime was terrible and had to be overthrown.[15] This unfortunate law was revoked in December 1973 but by then it was too late: the officer corps had solidified, the planning was far gone, and the realization that something would have to be done would not disappear. By late 1973 there was a group of approximately 200 officers who were involved in the planning of a coup, and it is important to note that the only key figure who had any political background was Major Melo Antunes. Others with political backgrounds, such as Vasco Gonçalves and Varela Gomes, were marginal to the planning. This was not a case of a few political types or Communist sympathizers leading the others. Rather, with the background sketched above, the catalyst of Law #353, and mainly because of the ongoing wars and the inability of the regime to respond intelligently, the group came to the conclusion that if the government could not end the war they would end the regime.[16]

General Spínola had an indirect role in the coup. He had been the superior officer in Guinea of many in the group and had ongoing discussions with them about the regime and the problem of the colonies. The still-forming MFA group referred to him as "our general," although Otelo Saraiva de Carvalho, the key figure in the group, had his differences with the general.[17] We can say that both the MFA and General Spínola evolved in their political plans through these discussions but did not come to an agreement on the need for, let alone the details of, a coup. The publication of the general's book, *Portugal and the Future,* was extremely important in the decision to overthrow the regime. The fact that such a prestigious officer, indeed the most prestigious officer, would publicly raise the question of the future of Portugal and the colonies was in itself a bombshell. It brought into the open and thus legitimated, at least in the eyes of the people, debate on Portugal's colonial future which, we must remember, was not even allowed as a topic of discussion in the 1973 elections to the National Assembly. It thus further supported the officers' questioning and criticisms of the regime vis-à-vis the colonies and the wars to retain them. Then, the regime's response by removing Generals Spínola and Costa Gomes from office highlighted its extreme intransigence. Marcelo Caetano, in allowing Spínola's book to be published in the first place, may have been seeking a degree of discussion (as he indicated early in his tenure in 1969) so as to prepare for some kind of negotiations. If this was the case, however, the reaction of the regime "ultras" indicated that he had no power at all, for in the National Assembly on March 5, 1974, he made a speech defending the colonial policy and the ongoing wars and received an oath of loyalty from the assembled 120 generals and admirals. For the MFA this was the final proof that a coup was the only solution to the regime and the wars. If the regime could not show any flexibility this was all the evidence required indicating that it was anachronistic, intolerable, and had to be overthrown.[18]

By mid-March there was barely sufficient unity and agreement within the MFA for a coup. There was, however, a certain urgency in that the regime was aware of the plotting and began to transfer key elements to missions outside of Metropolitan Portugal. Due to a problem of communications, and possible disagreement over strategy, there was a frustrated attempt at a coup by the regiment in Caldas de Rainha on March 15. The response by the regime, however, suggested to the MFA that with an increase in planning their coup would undoubtedly be successful. By this time it was clear that the regime lacked popular support, and its security apparatus of the DGS (secret police) and GNR (paramilitary force) was inade-

quate to quell a coup by the regular armed forces. The key plot-
ters were surprised by the high level of support both within the
military and among their contacts in the civilian population.
They speculated that it would not be necessary to involve
higher-level officers such as General Spínola in the post-coup
government to gain popular recognition and support. However, by this time agreements had been made and it was too
late to change.[19] This fact and the perception of their own capa-
bilities and support would, however, provide the basis for severe conflicts with Spínola and other superior officers once the
MFA succeeded with the coup.

The coup of April 25, 1974, which brought to an end the
regime founded by Oliveira Salazar almost half a century before and would open Portugal to revolutionary changes, was a
straightforward military operation in which there were no apparent snags. For a group of middle-level officers with tremendous experience in operations planning and conducting war in
Africa, this was a simple task—once the general support
within the military was ascertained. The emphasis was still on
the military plan for the coup as the MFA could not know in
advance that it would prove to be so simple. Major Otelo Saraiva de Carvalho was in charge of the military planning, and
his book *Alvorada em Abril* provides extensive detail on the
military preparation and operation.

The Post-coup Program of the MFA

Political planning for the coup was more limited for this
planning was done by officers only. From all the evidence I
have been able to gather (books by participants, interviews,
and secondary analyses) there were no civilians directly involved in the coup. Some were aware that plotting was going
on, knew a bit about the principal instigators, and had an idea
of the program, but this was exclusively a military operation.
The political section of the MFA was led by Majors Melo Antunes and Victor Alves who had relatively more political experience than the others with the exception of Brigadier General
Vasco Conçalves who came late to the MFA.[20] Melo Antunes
wrote several drafts of a program, and the main outlines were
approved by the larger group of the MFA. General Spínola received the Program on April 25 and demanded a number of
changes if he was to assume the formal leadership of the post-

coup government.[21] The Program itself, and the fact that General Spínola was able to demand significant changes at the last moment, are suggestive of what would happen during the ensuing two years, the most obvious of which suggests that the MFA promised too much, lacked political experience, and that serious difficulties would arise between the MFA which made the coup and General Spínola who was brought in to front it.

The Program of the MFA was broadcast to the nation on April 26, 1974. It is a short but comprehensive document and included the following provisions:[22] The MFA recognized that Portugal was in crisis and attributed this in large part to the wars in Africa. The *sine qua non* for any improvement in Portugal was a political solution to the wars. They indicated how the old regime would be dismembered in its structures and immediate democratization and serious socioeconomic changes would be forthcoming. While destroying the old regime, the MFA promised an expansion of mobilization, pluralism, and reforms which could amount to a revolution. These covered almost all possible topics, if not in detail at least by implication, following upon dismantling the Estado Novo, and the promise of what came to be known as the three "D's": Decolonization, Democratization, and Development.

It remains unclear even today why the MFA linked democratization to the political settlement of the wars and social reform. Documents and secondary evidence provide little insight on this key point, which distinguishes the MFA coup from other progressive military movements which have promised and even implemented social reforms, but have at most only rhetorically included democratization. The regimes I have in mind include Nasser's coup in 1952 and the Peruvian coup in 1968 and exclude those scores of coups that are obviously conservatively-oriented. Ordinarily progressive military coups result in some degree of reform but little democratization unless, as happened in Peru, they lose control and are forced to seek a civilian solution.[23] Judging from the available evidence, the MFA officers thought that the promise of democratization would solve a number of problems related to both decolonization and the crisis in Portugal. The old regime was not democratic, it was colonialist and intransigent. Democratization seemed to be a way to generate support for the "loss of Africa" and give the Portuguese a very different system from what they had suffered under for so long. Decolonization was undoubtedly the key element in the Program; Development and Democratization were defined and included to contrast the MFA and its emergent government with the old regime.

The Program was extremely ambitious. There are at least two general reasons for this beyond the above-mentioned desire to contrast the MFA to the old regime. First, the Program was not a succinct and coherent position statement, but rather more of a collage of political platforms and statements which had been issued during the preceding five years in Portugal. There were some elements from the Socialist Party (PS) platform, some from the PCP-oriented CDE, and even a few from a liberal group.[24] Thus while the military plan for the coup was well-planned and executed, the political statement was fragmented. Second, this was the case again for two reasons: first, the best single book on the preparation for and execution of the coup is subtitled *229 Days to Overthrow Fascism*.[25] This book, and other books written by participants, are unanimous in pointing out that this was not a coherent group which formed the MFA, and from the time of the publication of *Portugal and the Future* they were in a rush to bring off the coup before key elements were posted abroad or imprisoned. Because of this urgency the political plan necessarily took second place to the military undertaking. The Program, then, did not represent a document which had been hammered out over a long period by a cohesive group. The second reason is that even if they had spent more time and attention on the Program it is unlikely that the MFA could have formulated a political document representing the thought out and agreed-upon political ideas of more than a few dozen officers. What became obvious very quickly, and has been highlighted repeatedly in books and interviews by those involved, was the lack of political preparation of all but a handful in the MFA.[26] These were military officers who had spent all of their careers in this environment and much of this time on successive tours of duty in Africa. At least for this period in Portuguese history, the officers were too busy fighting wars to sit around the barracks thinking up coup attempts. Then, too, they were part of a society which discouraged politics and where the regime had most aspects of state and society under control. Political action was not a common occupation in Portugal. The Program with all its promises, which, it must be emphasized, were taken seriously by the MFA is largely due to the political naiveté of the key elements, the haste with which it was formulated, and the intention to contrast themselves and their post-coup government with the military coup of 1926 and the subsequent Salazar regime.

Post-coup Dynamics: Politics and the MFA

The main focus for understanding politics during the year 1974–75 was the relationship between the MFA and General Spínola. This was particularly true since the Program via the MFA dismantled the old regime, which was moribund and practically fell apart of its own accord. The structures of "representation" were abolished or intervened, the National Assembly closed, the DGS and censorship done away with in Metropolitan Portugal, the political movement (ANP) abolished, and indeed the elite most identified with the old regime became marginalized. Yet there was no new system to replace the decaying, discredited, and now demolished old regime. Since political parties had been forbidden, the emergent ones were either formerly clandestine (as the PCP) or new and weak (PS). In any case, the MFA lacked a system or a series of structures on which to build a new regime; the PCP did attempt to do so but through the intermediary of the MFA. As the structures on which to construct a new regime did not exist, the pivot became the relationship between the MFA and General Spínola.

As middle-level officers who had overthrown a long-established regime, the MFA did not feel adequate to rule on their own. Therefore they pulled back from direct involvement in public office and called upon General Spínola and other higher-level officers to form a Junta of National Salvation. General Spínola assumed an increasingly important role and began to make obvious what was realized from at least 1972: he wanted to be president and rule the country. Some astute observers realized this before April 25 along with the possibility that General Spínola might well outmaneuver the MFA. However, with the MFA's emphasis on hierarchy, doubts about their own ability to rule, and absence of established political parties, there was no option but to have someone like General Spínola assume the front position.[27] General Spínola and those around him were more in tune with the old regime than the MFA came to perceive itself to be. The process, which became one of conflict, contained a number of elements including age, rank, style, and relationship with the old regime. There were also major policy differences in that the MFA increasingly favored substantial changes in line with the Program, whereas General Spínola was much less eager to see full decolonization, major changes in Portugal, and a strong involvement by the population in politics. As Spínola, and the governments he headed (I and II Provisional Governments) occupied what could be termed a post-coup Right, the MFA defined itself in contrast and thus occupied the Left. Through a series of important policy issues Spínola was harried from the Left and resisted until he left the government completely in September 1974. However, he and his group were involved in an aborted coup on March 11, 1975, an incident which provided the quantum leap both in political and socioeconomic terms. That is, the high points of the definition of the MFA and the radicalization of the revolution are centered on the increasingly conflictual relations between General Spínola and the MFA. It is here that is found the main pivot to the political system during the first year after April 25.[28]

If initially the MFA allowed itself to be upstaged by General Spínola, something similar occurred regarding the political parties already formed or nascent. The coup, to repeat once again, was exclusively a military affair.[29] At the time of the coup the leader of the newly-founded Socialist Party (PS), Mario Soares, was in Bonn and the General Secretary of the PCP, Alvaro Cunhal, remained in exile in Prague. Even while drawing on party platforms and statements, the MFA Program did not stipulate the formation of political parties. Rather, "there will be permitted the formation of 'political associations,' possible embryos of future political parties. . . ."[30] Immediately, however, clandestine parties, the PS in exile, and new ones claimed the right to function as political parties. The MFA accepted them as indeed they had to accept General Spínola assuming a predominant role in government. Three months after the coup there were some 50 groups formed, mobilized, and competing with one another; these were normally much more than embryos and created a momentum for political involvement and radicalization. By the time the elections for the Constituent Assembly were held on April 25, 1975, there were 12 major parties. It is worth noting that only four of these were to the Right of the PCP (PS, PPD, CDS, PPM).[31] In order to further define the political context and some of the key actors we must, if only briefly, look at the PCP and the PS, the main parties in this period of MFA-Spínola radicalization.

Since the formal establishment of the Estado Novo in 1933 political parties had been illegal, and the União Nacional (later Acção Nacional Popular) was a movement rather than a party. The elections to the National Assembly in 1969 involved movements or associations rather than parties. The presidential elections, indirect since 1959 when the opposition candidate, General Humberto Delgado, apparently did too well, did not allow for party participation either. Parties, then, had to operate either clandestinely or in exile.

The Portuguese Communist Party was founded in 1921 and had been illegal since 1926. It survived in a clandestine existence and continued to publish *Avante*.[32] At the time of elections it worked through the CDE (later MDP/CDE) and was able to generate support in the southern agricultural regions and among organized industrial workers. In the latter group or class it was able, by 1974, to control union organizations, which the regime could not eliminate. While surviving and thus serving as something of a testimonial for organization and coherence even in a dictatorship as tight as the Estado Novo, the party underwent power splits, factions, and threats from the Left, as did other Communist parties. Still, the party had an heroic past, and in particular the characteristics of a Communist party of organization and ideology would serve it well after April 25, 1974.

The Socialist Party can trace its history back to the last century, but with less continuity and cohesion.[33] As an organization the more accurate date would be 1969, when those who would later form the PS created the CEUD in opposition to the PCP-dominated CDE for the elections to the National Assembly. To be precise, the PS was founded only in April 1973 in Bonn, Federal Republic of Germany, with support from the Friedrich Ebert Foundation. At the time of the coup the party was a name, a certain tradition of democratic socialism in Portugal, a link with the German SPD and the Socialist International, and a small group of cadres. It was most certainly not a coherent and organized party. The other groups which would become parties came out of these two, as well as some individuals, groups such as SEDES, and even the old regime.[34]

In the conflict between the MFA and General Spínola the political parties became, paradoxically enough, both more and less important. They became less important as the MFA became increasingly captivated with the idea of institutionalizing itself. From the original Program and the promise of democratization and elections, they fell back substantially and defined an ongoing role which would see them controlling or at least monitoring the political situation for years to come. Thus, rather than allowing General Spínola to hold power, or encouraging the political parties to interact and create dissent, or turning-back the revolution, they—the MFA—would rule and provide the conscious orientation they argued the country required. The process can be illustrated by their escalating conflicts with General Spínola and defined by the formation of different organizations. These began with the Coordinating Commission of the Program, which then became the Coordinating Commission of the MFA and finally the Council of Twenty. The high point in institutionalization was reached after March 11, 1975, when in reaction to the aborted coup from the Right, the highest powers were concentrated in an exclusively military Supreme Council of the Revolution which combined the powers of the Junta of National Salvation and the Council of Twenty. What is more, it also assumed powers previously held by the Joint Chiefs of Staff. The broader military organization, the Council of 200, became the Armed Forces Assembly with 240 members. These two organs, which overlapped to a significant degree with the provisional governments, held power and indicated this was to be a military system. The ongoing justification for this large role was provided in a Party Pact signed with the main parties, which in exchange for holding the election to the Constituent Assembly on April 25, 1975, recognized that the MFA would maintain a supervisory role over politics for a period of three to five years. This Pact was signed on April 2, thereby laying the foundation and granting a certain legal justification for the MFA's domination of the political system.[35]

However, while the MFA directed politics they did allow parties to function and held the elections to the Constituent Assembly as scheduled on April 25, 1975. Party activity continued, but the parties—particularly the PCP, and to a lesser extent, the PS—became more vigorous and assumed more importance after the radicalization of the MFA in the fall of 1974. The PS was involved during this period only because it was in general agreement with the PCP on issues which contrasted the MFA and General Spínola. Some six months later, in early 1975, over a single union system, and again in mid-1975 over the República affair, the PS and the PCP would be in complete opposition. During most of 1974 this was not the case.

My argument is that the MFA radicalized not because of certain individuals such as Vasco Gonçalves who became prominent and might have been Communist sympathizers, but because the PCP provided an organization and an ideology which suited the MFA. In the conflict between General Spínola and the MFA the former increasingly relied on support and legitimacy from elements remaining in the old regime, while the latter drew support and interpretations from the PCP. The PCP had been the main organizational opponent of the old regime, had a glorious history, and considering its ideology, an even more glorious future. In post-coup Portugal the PCP enjoyed legitimacy, an organization, and cadre with which to build a new Portugal as the old one was so obviously flawed, anachronistic, and without popular support. Immediately after the coup, on May 1 to be precise, the PCP sought to identify itself with the MFA. As the conflict between the MFA and General Spínola became increasingly heated and intractable, the former could look to the PCP for support and justification. Increasingly, somewhat similar to Cuba, a party was able to lend a certain cachet of radicalization to what had begun as a reformist movement. The PCP did this through a series of events and by means of a few very effective strategies.

The PCP took advantage of events such as General Spínola's "march of the silent majority" in September 1974, the debate over the structure of trade unions, and the attempted Rightist coup of March 11, 1975, to ingratiate itself with the MFA and push for a particular orientation to the revolution. It is likely that it was instrumental in promoting other events with the same goal: these would include the Party Pact of April 1975, and the seizure of the Socialist-oriented newspaper, *República,* in May 1975. The PCP was anxious to lend an organization and an interpretation to the MFA, which was moving increasingly to the Left in its struggle with General Spínola and elements thought to be identified with him and the old regime.

This approximation to the MFA was the most important strategy used by the PCP. Initially its prestige was great because of the Communists' ongoing opposition to the regime which had just collapsed. The PCP made extremely effective propaganda from this fact by continually referring to the number of years PCP members had spent in Salazar's prisons, to those who died in opposing the regime, and to their long, hard, and clandestine work with the industrial workers and peasants in the southern agricultural regions.[36] The PCP followed a very definite tactic of never criticizing or opposing the MFA. While other parties to its Left and Right became increasingly critical in 1975, the PCP studiously avoided any behavior which might create a gap between it and the MFA. Relations were particularly good during the premiership of Vasco Gonçalves between July 1974 and September 1975, and one can argue that Alvaro Cunhal was the second most important political figure in the country because of his close contacts with the premier. The PCP, with its persuasive ideology, heroic background, and close contacts with elements in the MFA was able to consolidate and enlarge its influence in the regime in general despite the absence or paucity of any Communists in the MFA. It took control over the Fifth Division and the Institute of Military Sociology where it published documents and reports, gave courses, and provided orientation to campaigns both within and without the military. Thus it was not only enlarging its influence, but also giving the appearance of being the key organization in this post-coup regime which lacked its own ideology and was seeking to resolve its own internal factions.

Another strategy utilized by the PCP was the participation in the provisional governments at the level of ministries and state secretaries. The First Provisional Government which was formed in May 1974 included two Communists: Alvaro Cunhal as Minister without Portfolio and Avelino Pacheco Gonçalves as Minister of Labor. More or less the same pattern applied right through the six provisional governments which ended only in July of 1976. There was some benefit to the PCP in holding these posts, for at least it knew what was being discussed and planned in the governments. However, there were drawbacks as well, not only because the governments were unstable and weak, but more importantly because the PCP undoubtedly lost prestige for having to assume positions in government which were not fully in line with its ideology. This was most obvious in situations regarding strikes and wages, and it seems convincing that General Spínola invited the Communists to participate in the First Provisional Government precisely to force them to accept responsibility during a period which would obviously be quite difficult.[37]

A third strategy was the PCP's control of much of the media. Television and the government radio network was under its control as were the most important daily newspapers, including *Diário de Noticias, O Século,* and *Diário de Lisboa.* It did not, however, monopolize all of the media. The Church maintained a radio station, which was taken over for a period by the far Left, and there were stations in Porto as well. There were at least two daily papers not under PCP control (*A República* and *Jornal Novo*) and a number of weeklies with very different orientations. It should be noted that some of the papers were specifically formed to provide a different view from the official media. Again, this role in the media gave the impression of greater PCP control and more radical revolutionary processes than would have otherwise been the case.

A fourth strategy concerns the influence of the PCP within the state apparatus. This applied in particular to the ministries of Labor, Agriculture, and Communications. The legislation promoted by these ministries, and to some degree implemented, sought to duplicate a model of society similar to those in the planned and centralized economies. Again, these policies stimulated from above the revolutionary process which was also being promoted from below. The PCP never did control the whole state apparatus, and by mid-1975 its policies were being countered by both the far Left and the Right.

The fifth and sixth strategies did not seek to influence the regime or the society, as did the previous four. Rather, they dealt with the bases of both. One was the tactic with the MDP/CDE in which they jointly took over local governments. During previous elections the MDP/CDE was an electoral front in which the PCP played a predominant role, and this coalition continued after the revolution despite arguments to the contrary. As the old regime collapsed, these were the only local political groups existing which were not identified with the regime and they took over local bodies such as the "grémios da lavoura, juntas de freguesias, and camaras municipais." The other strategy was to do the same thing with the labor movement. Under the old regime the unions were official and controlled, although the PCP was making substantial inroads before 1974. With the coup it simply took over the national organizations and consolidated its hold within the unions. This would be the one area where the PCP continued to hold power long after it had been forced to retreat on other sides. Of course, this was precisely the area where the PCP had the greatest amount of background and preparation. The other five strategies were possible because of the revolutionary ferment (in some high degree promoted by the PCP) and the absence of other competent political organizations during the first year or so of the revolution.

The importance of these strategies in the context of a regime which had collapsed in the face of a military coup, a situation in which the MFA felt unprepared to rule and turned over power to General Spínola with whom they would then conflict, was the fact that the PCP went very far in implementing its model of modernization. I personally do not know if the PCP was intending to "go all the way for hegemonic power." There are indications either way, and as regards a party which has always been extremely close to Moscow one cannot evaluate the PCP's actions without considering the broader concerns of the USSR.[38] It is evident that the PCP was seeking to revolutionize the society: to implement a model of modernization very different from that guaranteed under the old regime. Some sense of this can be gained by a brief review of a few key events of 1975.

The most important issue of early 1975 was whether the PCP would be allowed to control the national labor movement. In October 1970 the PCP had formed Intersindical as a parallel union structure which was illegal but tolerated, and after April 25 the PCP took over most of the movement and put Intersindical in command. From January 1975 it was undecided as to whether this would be the only legally recognized organization since the Socialists, and others to a lesser degree, were also forming unions. After much discussion and even more polemic, the post-March 11 Supreme Council of the Revolution, the highest military body and thus most powerful, decided in favor of the PCP and Intersindical. Therefore, as far as labor organizations and the relationship of unionized workers to the state was concerned, the PCP achieved its goal.

The aborted Rightist coup of March 11 was important for the PCP. Immediately General Spínola, as well as the Center and the Right, were eclipsed; the whole spectrum of politics moved considerably to the Left. What is more, the government organs were weakened as the Revolutionary Council and the Assembly of the MFA became predominant. The latter organization included noncommissioned officers and men from the ranks who were elected as were the officers of the Revolutionary Council. Since military hierarchy was breaking down and the PCP had influence through control of key areas in the military, it took advantage of the elections. The bodies became radical indeed. The immediate policies after the attempted coup of

March 11 reflected this radicalization in that the banks and then the insurance companies were nationalized. This was extremely important not only because it involved control of the economy, but also because it extended formal control of the state over most of the newspapers. With these major nationalizations accomplished, other nationalizations, expropriations, and simply takeovers without regard to the laws were performed.[39] Rapidly, then, the economy became nationalized and under the direct control of the state, although in the first instance possibly under the control of the workers. These policies superseded in one swoop the pro-Socialist economic plan known as the "Programa de Política, Económica, e Social," which had been announced on February 21 by Major Melo Antunes after months of preparation and discussion.

After March 11 the most important event was the signing of the Party Pact by the MFA and the six main political parties on April 11. This Pact institutionalized the role of the MFA and although following on discussions prior to March 11, it in some respects contradicted the Program of the MFA. It meant that the elections to the Constituent Assembly on April 25, 1975, were somewhat superfluous, for the MFA would continue to play the predominant role in politics for the next three to five years. Inasmuch as the strategy of the PS and parties to its Right had to be based on an electoral strategy, their basis for power disappeared. The PCP, on the other hand, realizing that its probable electoral support was far less than its control through other strategies, could only benefit particularly in light of its links with the MFA. Therefore, the Party Pact indicated that Portugal would not pursue the normal liberal democratic pattern but would in some way be "guided."

Undoubtedly the high point in the consolidation of the PCP model of modernization was the document entitled "Documento-Guia-Aliança Povo-MFA" (Basic Document for the Alliance of the People and the MFA) of July 8. Whereas the events of March 11 superseded the Programa of February 21, this Document superseded the "Plana de Ação Política" (PAP-Political Action Plan) of June 21. This PAP was prepared largely by Major Melo Antunes and emerged from the Revolutionary Council. It was definitely progressive, characterized the MFA as a liberation movement, and stipulated that socialism in Portugal would be attained in a pluralistic manner. It received the support of the PS which brought that party closer to some "moderate" elements in the MFA (to be discussed below). The

Documento was prepared by the cabinet of the Fourth Provisional Government and presented by Premier Vasco Gonçalves not to the Revolutionary Council, but to the much more radical Assembly of the MFA, where it was passed on July 8. What was particularly important about this Documento was its provision for a vanguard to lead the revolution; this vanguard was to be the military, and judging from the MFA Assembly, it would be strongly influenced by the PCP.

By early July 1975, then, the PCP and its supporters in the MFA had gained predominant control in the apparatus of state, the media, and key organizations at the bases. Its approach to modernization was increasingly adopted at official levels, and through control of much of the media was promoted throughout the society. The PCP and its supporters in the MFA did not have complete authority over the armed forces, but in the revolutionary momentum their strategies were not opposed. However, in the process of politicization and in the absence of a single agreed upon regime, the PCP was increasingly opposed from the Right and Left. From the Left it was assailed by Maoists, Anarchists, Trotskyites, and various other forms of "nonrevisionist" ideological groups. On the Right it was increasingly harassed by the PS and the PPD.[40] That is, the conditions allowing it to gain such power also limited this power for virtually everything was up for grabs in this chaotic situation in which the MFA was politically inept and not unified. The limitation on the PCP and its allies which would become obvious by late 1975 is most effectively analyzed by regarding the PS and the MFA itself.

In the elections to the Constituent Assembly on April 25, 1975, the PS received 37.9 percent, the PPD 26.3 percent, and the PCP 12.5 percent.[41] Since the PS did not possess the grassroots organization of the PCP, the cadres, nor for that matter a clear ideology, it had no option but to argue for a liberal democratic regime where votes would be the main criteria. What is more, it was closely affiliated with the strand of democratic socialism represented in the Social Democratic parties of northern Europe. Initially, after April 25, 1974, the PS was close to the PCP but by the time of a debate over a single union and the subsequent Party Pact they had moved very far apart indeed. With the results of the elections the PS argued, with some justification, that the people clearly favored a liberal democratic system and in this system the PS was the main party. Their argument on the former point was based not only on the low vote for the PCP, but the extremely low blank vote of 7 percent which was requested by some in the MFA as a sign that the people wanted the MFA and not parties. Additionally, the turn-out for the elections was an astonishing 92 percent. In making their point, the Socialists held meetings and demonstrations throughout the country and emphasized that the commitment to democracy was stated in the MFA Program. The most important reaction to this was the takeover of *República* by the far-left oriented workers in mid-May which embarrassed the PCP. When the Revolutionary Council and the "intervention force of the military" (COPCON) of Otelo Saraiva de Carvalho were not able to return the paper to the Socialists, they withdrew from the Fourth Provisional Government on July 10 leading to the collapse of the government a week later. This was a period of severe strife with frequent demonstrations and a great deal of posturing and threats.

The PS was able to participate in this dissension because it was beginning to take shape as a party. Having been founded only in 1973, by 1975 it began to resemble other sister parties in Europe. This occurred in large measure because of extensive assistance from these parties, which included the moral support of visits by such leaders of democratic socialism as Willy Brandt, Olaf Palme, Bruno Kreisky, Daniel Mayer, and Den Uyl. Probably more important, however, was the more concrete support, which included funds and personnel as well as training and techniques so that the PS could function as an organization as quickly as possible to compete with the PCP. It is doubtful that the PS could compete in the revolutionary context with deteriorating relations with most of the MFA, had it not been for another strategy involving the PS and the sister parties. It was obvious that Portugal would need loans and credits if it was to avoid economic catastrophe. This realization was reflected in the opposition (to the PCP) press and in documents from sectors in the MFA. However, Portugal's appeals for loans were met with indifference by lending agencies, governments, and the EEC—with a few minor exceptions—and it was made clear in private and public that Portugal could not count on economic support from the West unless it established a "pluralistic political system." This message was passed through the Socialist International, the EEC, and a number of states. It is difficult to know how coordinated or orchestrated the strategy was, but there is no doubt in my mind that it was indeed a well thought-out and implemented plan.[42] This meant, of course, that Portugal could not be dominated either by the PCP nor by the MFA in some kind of tutelary or guided democracy. It had to be an electorally-based, functioning liberal democracy much in line with other European systems. In sum, the PS strategy of opposing the PCP and fighting for recognition of the election results as the basis for governing was linked to an external strategy which would constrain Portugal severely unless the PS goal was achieved. Obviously the PPD was in accord with this goal, as were some of the minor parties which also opposed the PCP from either Right or Left.

During the period from late–1974 until 1976, political parties, even the highly organized and strategy-oriented PCP, were secondary actors in the political struggle. The parties during this time, first the PCP and then the PS, advanced and receded depending on the dynamics of the MFA. A certain mutual influence or interaction was evident, but the prime mover was clearly the MFA. In general, but with some notable exceptions such as Otelo Saraiva de Carvalho, Diniz de Almeida, and Carlos Fabião, the founding elements of the MFA became identified as a "moderate" line in opposition to Premier Vasco Gonçalves and the radicalizing elements of the PCP and the Assembly of the MFA.[43] These moderates supported the Melo Antunes Programa of February 21 and his Plano of June 21. They were, however, overshadowed in politics as they were otherwise engaged in foreign affairs and in the ministries dealing with socioeconomic matters. These moderates were thus somewhat politically marginal, and, in that context of politicization in general and especially in the armed forces, were not secure in their military support. Certain events, in part defined by the international constraints just discussed, brought them together and allowed them to broaden their support, join with the PS for a time, force out Vasco Gonçalves, and halt the increasing influence of the PCP.

This group recognized the implications of the elections, the strategy of the PS, and the reaction by the PCP and elements in the MFA itself. They were particularly bothered by the attacks on the leader of the PS, Mario Soares, at the May 1 celebration and the takeover of República. Even though some apparently sympathized with the PCP's model of modernization, they realized it would not work in Portugal for both domestic and external reasons. Domestically, the country would not accept the model without a great deal of force. Quite possibly Lisbon and the south were radical, but the populous important northern half of the country was known to be conservative. The north's reaction to the radicalization in Lisbon became manifest in the violence which began in June 1975 and was directed against PCP offices. The high point was probably reached on July 13 when civilians cut communications at Rio Maior, thus defining the break between north and south of Portugal. Some of the violence may well have been encouraged by political parties of the Right and even foreigners, and was in many cases abetted by the Church, but the anti-Communist feelings of the people were certainly genuine and became stronger the closer the PCP came to power. Externally, or internationally, it would not work because Portugal was part of Western Europe, a member of NATO, and very far from the sphere of the Red Army. As military men, this group knew full well that if a Communist government came to power in Portugal it would not last long. And when it fell, Rightist groups such as the MDLP and ELP would be waiting to step in, pick up the pieces, and quickly reimpose a system similar to the one the MFA overthrew on April 25, 1974.[44] There was thus an increasing consensus that the PCP and its supporters in the MFA must be put down. This consensus was cemented by the approval in the Assembly of the MFA of the Documento in early July and the fall of the Fourth Provisional Government in the middle of the month. The moderates realized that in the ensuing confusion the PCP could achieve more power, and thus they were obliged to step in. The final catalyst was a specifically military threat.

Even before the coup of April 25, 1974, but certainly after it, discipline in the armed forces was disintegrating. A coup brought off by middle-level officers against their superiors and the regime was contrary to military tradition and discipline. The conflict with General Spínola led to further erosions of discipline, particularly as most of those around the General were superior to the officers of the MFA. And, as noted above, the PCP through the Fifth Division and the military institutes intentionally sought to radicalize the military. Movements to the Left of the PCP were also at work on the military such as the PRP-BR which influenced the very important intervention force—COPCON. Thus one could say that the power of the MFA Assembly, which was elected and included noncoms and privates, more or less accurately reflected the overall situation in the armed forces by the summer of 1975: the so-called "Hot

Summer of 1975."[45] Insofar as the moderates in the MFA, or any officer not identified with the PCP or a more radical party, had a power base it had to be in the military as institution. As the institution disintegrates, that power base disappears. What is more, civil war also becomes possible as the institution weakens and fragments. Despite the supposed institutionalization of the MFA, personalities remained extremely important. This is clear not only by the nature of the material published by those involved—which is mainly personal testimony—but also secondary materials and newspaper reports.[46] The main factions after General Spínola's departure on March 11 were those around Major Melo Antunes, drafter of the original Program of the MFA and most other documents, and Brigadier General Vasco Gonçalves who entered the MFA late, became premier, and was close to Alvaro Cunhal. With the radicalization in the spring of 1975, the division between Melo Antunes and Vasco Gonçalves became increasingly apparent.[47] Two groups formed: those known as the moderates around the former; the radicals and the government around the latter.

The action which impressed the moderates with the disintegration of the military as institution and their obligation to step in before it was too late, was the subverting of the Commando regiment at Amadora outside Lisbon. This regiment was one of the elite units in the country and when it mutinied and forced its commander, Colonel Jaime Neves, out on July 31, they realized matters were indeed serious. Through the intercession of the mercurial General Otelo Saraiva de Carvalho the commander was reinstated. The moderates then defined a strategy, and Melo Antunes wrote a document known as the "Document of the Nine," which was published on August 7. In this Document the moderates come out against Premier Vasco Gonçalves, oppose the model of modernization and strategy of the PCP, analyze problems of politics and of the economy, and return to their original Program of the MFA as reiterated in the PAP of June 21. The group and the Document was supported publicly by the PS and other parties to its Right, while being vociferously attacked by those to the Left. This Document provided the basis for uniting large sectors of the armed forces and bringing them into closer contact with civilian elements who obviously supported the restated commitment to a liberal democratic regime. The publication of the "Document of the Nine" resulted in the collapse of the Fifth Provisional

Government, the loss of support of the premier, and finally his removal from governmental and military roles in late August. This provided the basis for the formation of another Provisional Government, the Sixth, which would more accurately reflect the new coalition of forces in which the PCP was on the defensive, the military radicals also hesitant, and the other major political parties on the rise. However, the situation would be mediated or defined by the moderates in the MFA who, while having the power to force out Vasco Gonçalves, might not be able to bring the whole military situation under control particularly when the other political parties lacked the strength and organizational coherence of the PCP. It would, then, be a difficult task to fully define the new regime. One option was eliminated, but the important issue was still to come.

Not only did the question of regime remain to be defined, but so was the type of socioeconomic system that this regime would implement. Until August 1975 at least four major documents (two by Melo Antunes and two by groups further to the Left) and probably a dozen less important proposed models and strategies whereby Portugal would modernize. It was clear that the old regime's pattern of (non) modernization was moribund, but there was little agreement as to what path Portugal should follow in attempting to catch up with the rest of the world.

Notes

1. See, for example, the comments on this by one of the key participants in the MFA. Otelo Saraiva de Carvalho, *Alvorada em Abril* (Amadora: Livraria Bertrand, 1977), pp. 107–8.

2. On this see, for example, Keith Middlemas, *Cabora Bassa: Engineering and Politics in Southern Africa* (London: Weidenfeld and Nicolson, 1975), p. 319.

3. Avelino Rodrigues, et al., *O Movimento dos Capitães e o 25 de Abril: 229 Dias Para Derrubar o Fascismo* (Lisbon: Moraes Editores, 1974), pp. 276–83. Saraiva de Carvalho, *Alvorada em Abril*, also comments on this, pp. 178–80. For the views of some of those involved regarding Africa and the revolution, with reference to the topic of note 2 above, see J. da Luz Cunha, Kaulza de Arriaga, Bethencourt Rodrigues, and Silvino Silvério Marques, *Africa: A Vitória Traída* (Braga: Intervenção, 1977).

4. Rodrigues, *O Movimento dos Capitães*, pp. 245, 254.

5. Middlemas, *Cabora Bassa*, p. 317.

6. Marcello Caetano, *Depoimento* (Rio de Janeiro: Distribuidora Record, 1974), pp. 191–92.

7. Ibid., p. 196.

8. Saraiva de Carvalho, *Alvorada em Abril,* pp. 122–23. Rodrigues, *O Movimento dos Capitães,* p. 260. Of General Spínola's works see not only *Portugal e O Futuro* (n.p.: Arcadia, 1974) but also a series of interviews, speeches, and conferences published as *Ao Serviço de Portugal* (Lisbon: Atica/Bertrand, 1976).

9. For extensive data and analysis see Douglas L. Wheeler, "The Military and the Portuguese Dictatorship, 1926–1974: 'The Honor of the Army'," in *Contemporary Portugal: The Revolution and its Antecedents,* eds. Lawrence S. Graham and Harry M. Makler (Austin: University of Texas Press, 1979), pp. 191–220 and especially 201–2.

10. I sensed this shortly after the coup and discussed the point in my "The Portuguese Coup: Causes and Probable Consequences," *The World Today* (July 1974).

11. Rodrigues, *O Movimento dos Capitães,* pp. 341–54 provide an analysis of the class of the officers. Precisely this type of question is dealt with in Antonio Rangel Bandeira, "Military Interventions in Portuguese Politics," *Brazilian Studies* (Toronto: August 1975) 91 mimeographed pages.

12. Saraiva de Carvalho, *Alvorada em Abril,* p. 127, makes this point well. In fact all the personal comments on the causes of the coup make pretty much the same point. See the complicated, but rich in documentation, volumes by Diniz de Almeida, *Ascensão, Apogeu e Queda do MFA* (Lisbon: Edições Sociais, 1977? n.d.) in two volumes.

13. Saraiva de Carvalho, *Alvorada em Abril.* For some discussion on this point in response to an interviewer see Cap. Vasco Lourenço, *MFA: Rosto do Povo* (Lisbon: Portugália, n.d.).

14. Saraiva de Carvalho, *Alvorada em Abril,* p. 189. It should be pointed out that I rely heavily on Saraiva de Carvalho and Rodrigues, et al., as they bring together most of the points reasonably well. These same points are substantiated in the two or three dozen books or pamphlets (as Lourenço above) by those involved, or wanting to demonstrate that they had been involved. The same material can be found in the newspaper interviews.

15. Rodrigues, *O Movimento dos Capitães,* pp. 305–38.

16. For a good discussion on the background of the coup see also Lawrence S. Graham, "The Military in Politics: The Politicization of the Portuguese Armed Forces," in Graham and Makler, *Contemporary Portugal,* pp. 221–56. See also The Insight Team of the Sunday Times, *Insight on Portugal: The Year of the Captains* (London: Andre Deutsch, 1975), pp. 31–53.

17. This difference is expressed clearly in Otelo Saraiva de Carvalho, *Cinco Meses Mudaram Portugal* (Lisbon: Portugália, n.d.), pp. 19–20 for example.

18. For example, Saraiva de Carvalho, *Alvorada em Abril*, pp. 225–26.

19. Saraiva de Carvalho, *Alvorada em Abril*, speculates on this. See for example, pp. 467–86.

20. Ibid., p. 338. For some background on Melo Antunes see the quite disappointing book by M. Manuela de S. Rama and Carlos Plantier, *Melo Antunes: Tempo se Ser Firme* (Lisbon: Liber, 1976). Robert Harvey in *Portugal: Birth of a Democracy* (London: Macmillan Press, 1978) finds Melo Antunes behind all sorts of things and does not cast the Major in a very positive image.

21. Saraiva de Carvalho, *Alvorada em Abril*, p. 339. See also Avelino Rodrigues, et al., *Portugal Depois de Abril* (Lisbon: Intervoz, 1976), pp. 299–304 reproduce the various drafts of the document and the changes.

22. For the English version see Douglas Porch, *The Portuguese Armed Forces and the Revolution* (London: Croom Helm, 1977), Appendix III, pp. 244–47.

23. On Peru see, in particular, the comprehensive and excellent study by Alfred Stepan, *The State and Society: Peru in Comparative Perspective* (Princeton: Princeton University Press, 1978).

24. For a discussion of the elements of the Program see Rodrigues, *O Movimento dos Capitães*, pp. 224–27. Also, *Expresso*, 27 April 1974, provides a good discussion on the documents leading up to the Program.

25. Rodrigues, *O Movimento dos Capitães*.

26. The excellent introduction by Eduardo Lourenço to Saraiva de Carvalho, *Alvorada em Abril*, makes this point clearly. See also Sanches Osório, *O Equívoco de 25 de Abril* (Rio de Janeiro: Livraria Francisco Alves, 1975). Most of the personal testimonies make this point even if unintentionally.

27. Saraiva de Carvalho, *Cinco Meses Mudaram Portugal*, p. 75 for example.

28. Graham, "The Military in Politics," argues this same point. See also de Almeida, *Ascensão*, vol. 1, p. 48.

29. For discussions on relations with the parties see Rodrigues, *O Movimento dos Capitães*, pp. 222–30; Saraiva de Carvalho, *Alvorada em Abril*, pp. 312, 316, 334. See also Osório, *O Equívoco*, pp. 37, 38, 55.

30. This point is specifically discussed in Osório, *O Equívoco*, pp. 47–48.

31. There is much descriptive material on the political parties. See for example Antunes, Manual, Amorim, et al., *A Opção do Voto* (Lisbon: Intervoz, 1975), and SOAPLI, *Partidos e Movimentos Politicos em Portugal* (Lisbon: SOAPLI, 1975). See also Howard J. Wiarda, "Spain and Portugal," in *Western European Party Systems*, ed. Peter H. Merkl (New York: The Free Press, 1980), pp. 298–328.

32. There is some material on the PCP. See, for example, Arnold

Hottinger, "The Portuguese Communists," *Problems of Communism* (July-August 1975), pp. 1–17 and Eusebio M. Mujal-Leon, "The PCP and the Portuguese Revolution," *Problems of Communism* (January-February 1977): 21–41. For one of innumerable documents by the Secretary General see Álvaro Cunhal, *A Revolução Portuguesa: O Passado e o Futuro* (Lisbon: Edições Avante, 1976).

33. On the PS see Mario Soares, *Portugal's Struggle for Liberty* (London: George Allen & Unwin, 1975) (translated by Mary Gawsworth), and Mario Soares, Willy Brandt, and Bruno Kreisky, *Liberdade Para Portugal* (Amadora: Livraria Bertrand, 1976) also provides some background.

34. For some general information on the parties before 1974 see Herminio Martins, "Opposition in Portugal," *Government and Opposition*, 4 (Spring 1969): 250–63.

35. Of particular utility here is Graham, "The Military in Politics," pp. 221–56 and The Insight Team of the Sunday Times, *Insight on Portugal*, pp. 247–56. See also the stimulating interpretation on this period by Carlos E. de Medeiros Lino Gaspar, "Codes, Conspirations et Crises: Les Résurgences du Patrimonialisme et L'Evolution Démocratique Portugaise, 1974–1975," Mémoire du fin d'études du DEA Troisie Cycle d'Etudes Politiques Institut d'Etudes Politiques, Paris, 1982. This detailed analysis of the institutionalization of the MFA and its links with the population seeks a new interpretation of the dynamics of the MFA in light of the patrimonial model of politics.

36. This information, and not a little of the propaganda, can be found in Gil Green, *Portugal's Revolution* (N.Y.: International Publishers, 1976), and Wilfred Burchett, *Portugal Depois da Revolução dos Capitães* (Lisbon: Seara Nova, 1975). Both authors represent the orthodox Communist Party orientation.

37. The Insight Team of the Sunday Times, *Insight on Portugal*, p. 111.

38. The hegemonic pretensions are suggested in an interview with Armando de Castro by Dr. Mário Bacalhau in *Vida Mundial*, 23 October 1975. On the international dimensions see the very useful article by Joan Barth Urban, "Contemporary Soviet Perspectives on Revolution in the West," *Orbis* 19 (Winter 1976): 1359–1402. See also the very good article on the relationship with two sister parties, Alex Macleod, "The French and Italian Communist Parties and the Portuguese Revolution," in *In Search of Modern Portugal: The Revolution and Its Consequences*, eds. Lawrence S. Graham and Douglas L. Wheeler (Madison: Univ. of Wisconsin Press, 1983), pp. 297–320.

39. The single most useful compilation of the links and take-overs is M. Belmira Martins and J. Chaves Rosa, *O Grupo Estado* (Lisbon: Edições Expresso, 1979).

40. The Insight Team of the Sunday Times, *Insight on Portugal*, gives a good sense of this period. For more information see also Mar-

cio Moreira Alves, *Os Soldados Socialistas de Portugal* (Lisbon: Iniciativas Editoriais, 1975).

41. For a brief discussion of the elections see Ben Pimlott, "Parties and Voters in the Portuguese Revolution: The Elections of 1975 and 1976," *Parliamentary Affairs* 30 (1977): 35–58. For a long discussion see Juan Carlos Gonzales Hernandez, "El proceso electoral portugués. Analisis cuantitativo del comportamiento politico (1975–1976)," *REOP* 48 (1977): 205–70. For consistency, due to returns from non-Metropolitan Portugal and partial returns, I have used for all elections between 1975 and 1980 the *Atlas Eleitoral* (Lisbon: Editorial Progresso Social e Democracia, SARL, 1981).

42. On the economic situation see, for example, Paul Krugman and Jorge Braga de Macedo, "The Economic Consequences of the April 25th Revolution," in *Portugal Since the Revolution: Economic and Political Perspectives*, eds. Jorge Braga de Macedo and Simon Serfaty (Boulder, Colorado: Westview Press, 1981), pp. 53–87. Many of my interviews in Europe and North America dealt with this question of strategies as did all of those in the embassies in Lisbon.

43. Rodrigues, *Portugal Depois de Abril*, deals well with this theme. See also the "insider" account of José Gomes Mota, *A Resistência: O verão quente de 1975* (Lisbon: Edições Expresso, 1976).

44. There is little good literature on these movements and newspaper reporting is as useful as anything. See, however, the sensational Gunter Wallraff, *A Descoberta de uma Conspiração* (Lisbon: Bertrand, 1976) (translated from German).

45. See Mota, *A Resistência*, who uses this as a subtitle and analyzes the process of polarization.

46. This includes Mota, *A Resistência*, Rodrigues, *Portugal Depois de Abril*, de Almedia, *Ascensão*, and the Insight Team of the Sunday Times, *Insight on Portugal.*

47. de Almeida, *Ascensão*, vol. 1, pp. 296–69.

3

Modernization through Revolution: Observations on the Changes

The background to the changes which have been termed revolutionary is found in the specific history of Portugal and particularly the Estado Novo which sought to perpetuate both the colonial empire and the extremely backward economy and society. The revolutionary process unleashed by the coup of April 25, 1974, was caused by this backwardness and would bring about substantial changes in this situation. It must be emphasized, however, that the revolutionary process was based neither on a popular consensus nor on the power of an hegemonic party. Rather, the revolution is best visualized as a tremendous "leap ahead" in which structures of economy, polity, and society were thrown into the air, so to speak, without a coherent plan or program. Whereas a certain coherence was associated with traditional society, which was itself coming apart from economic change and social modernization, there was to be no coherence at all in the revolutionary process for it represented the disintegration of the old system in conjunction with varied and competing models proposed by newly formed political groups and movements. In this short chapter some of the main areas of change in Portugal will be briefly outlined. This is not intended as a comprehensive description, let alone analysis, of the changes brought about through revolution, but rather a categorization so that we might better understand regime-formation in a post-coup Portugal. It should be noted that José Medeiros Ferreira in his recent *Ensaio Histórico sobre a Revolução do 25 de Abril* follows a similar strategy to mine in first analyzing the political dynamics of the revolution and then giving some fairly brief indications of the social and economic changes which were brought about. The footnotes will provide suggestions for readings in order to better appreciate the scope of the changes and the Bibliography will give more comprehensive literature.

Undoubtedly the main change in the revolution, as well as its immediate cause, was the colonial empire. Portugal was both the first and last imperial power, having established its bases in southern Africa in the late fifteenth century and losing its colonies only in 1974 and 1975. It has convincingly been argued that Portugal was not the dominant power in the imperial system but rather its prisoner.[1] Modern Portugal was too small, weak, and economically underdeveloped to fully exploit its colonies. But, for these same reasons it could not afford to give them up, and Premier Oliveira Salazar frequently stated that Portugal without its Ultramar would not survive as an independent country. It was to be anticipated that there would be rapid and fundamental change in Portugal's relationship with the Ultramar, as this was the crux of the country's definition of itself and the cause of the coup. However, this in no way assumes that there would be agreement on the issue of the empire. Even before General Spínola agreed to head the successful movement which had overthrown the old regime, he demanded changes in the Program of the MFA and these concerned mainly the question of the empire. Then, after he assumed leadership in the First Provisional Government, it would be the colonial issue in particular which brought him into conflict with the MFA and the political parties and groups supporting it.[2] Whereas General Spínola apparently continued to believe in the feasibility of some kind of Lusitanian Federation, others wanted complete decolonization as rapidly as possible. As General Spínola's political base disappeared in the move to the Left by the MFA, the rapid decolonization would be affected. This was highlighted as early as July 27, 1974, in the political defeat of General Spínola's group as manifested in the resignation of Palma Carlos as premier. From this point it was clear that independence would be granted, and the negotiations concerned minor details rather than large issues. With a military tired of fighting, the regime committed to the empire overthrown, and an increasing optimism on the part of the guerrilla movement, it was manifestly impossible to consider anything but decolonization. The only questions remaining were those of timing and recognition of particular movements.

Independence for Guinea-Bissau came on September 10, 1974, thereby resolving an issue which was the single most important and immediate cause of the coup. The Lusaka Agreement between Portugal and Frelimo was reached on August 7, 1974, with independence for Mozambique on June 25, 1975. Independence for the Cape Verde Islands came on July 5, 1975, and for São Tome and Principe Island on July 12 of that same year. The largest problem of decolonization would involve the most important colony—Angola—both because of the size of the settler colony (300,000 plus) and the lack of a single unquestioned guerrilla movement. As the richest colony, Angola would represent a major loss and with the size of the population would involve negotiations to provide for the colonists' interests. The stakes were extremely high. Also, whereas the PAIGC in Guinea-Bissau and Frelimo in Mozambique held unquestioned power, this was not the case in Angola where the FNLA, MPLA, and UNITA fought each other and the Portuguese almost indiscriminately. What is more, the international issue of South Africa, the United States, and the Soviet Union would also confuse decolonization as was evidenced in the direct involvement of South Africa and Cuba and the indirect involvement (at the minimum) of the superpowers.[3]

Negotiations between Portugal and the three guerrilla movements began in October 1974, and an agreement was reached on January 10, 1975, known as the Alvor Agreement. In this Agreement independence was to be reached on November 11, 1975, after a period under a transitional government in which the Portuguese would play a role. Instead, civil war broke out in March 1975, the elections stipulated in the Agreement were never held, and the superpowers intervened. Finally, as the date of independence approached, Portugal was clearly without influence in the situation and was not able to recognize any of the movements. In its haste to get out as quickly as possible, sovereignty was turned over to "the people of Angola."

Quite simply, Portugal had stayed far too long in Africa and once a withdrawal was initiated it turned into a complete retreat. In the provisional governments of Portugal between July 1974 and September 1975 there was clear sympathy for the MPLA. This was particularly true during the tenure of Admiral Rosa Coutinho as High Commissioner for Angola. The final result was that after some 14 years of fighting to retain the colonies, Portugal was forced to leave under terms acceptable to no one in a situation of civil war. The decolonization may well have been exemplary in terms of speed, but not in terms of results. This would be particularly poignant in Portugal itself as the country had to receive approximately 500,000 "returnees" or refugees from the colonies. The colonial legacy would haunt Portugal for a number of years, although the civil war in Angola and the mass slaughter in Timor would not lead to the degree of violence at home that France had suffered after the independence of Algeria.[4] It seems likely that the international assistance for the refugees—in reaching Portugal, surviving there initially, and then becoming established through projects—particularly from the United States, was important in minimizing the violence and difficulty of (re)adjustment.

Of the many changes brought about by the revolution, the only one which is completely and totally irreversible is the process of decolonization. The others which will now be discussed are to some degree reversible.

One area of dramatic change brought about by the revolutionary process is the massive intervention of the state in the economy. Traditionally the Estado Novo through the "condiciamento economico" played a regulating role in the economy, but mainly in terms of politics and administration rather than investment or ownership.[5] At the height of the revolutionary fervor, following the aborted coup of March 11, 1975, the state moved into the economy. The economic power of the country was taken over by the political power. On March 14 the banks were nationalized (except for the Franco-Portuguese Credit Bank, the Portuguese departments of the Bank of London and South America, the Bank of Brazil, and the Agricultural Credit Banks), a fact which was doubly important since the trusts used banks as the bases of their extensive economic holdings; thus nationalization of the banks implied a series of other nationalizations. On March 15 the major insurance companies were also nationalized. In late March enterprises in tobacco, cement, and cellulose were nationalized. And, in April, the oil companies, railways, shipping companies, Portuguese Maritime Transport Company, and the airline—TAP—were also nationalized. In sum, in a period of approximately two months the "commanding heights of the economy were taken over by the state."[6]

The process of nationalization was haphazard, but a great deal of spontaneous or politically motivated takeover occurred as well, so that many firms were brought under worker control and then later taken over by the state. There are many variations on this process, but the final result was that the state assumed a larger role in the economy than would be indicated by the legal nationalizations of March and April 1975.[7] The OECD statistics indicating that the public sector in Portugal controls 24.4 percent of total value added and 45.5 percent of the total gross fixed capital formation are accurate as far as they go, but are somewhat misleading as the nationalizations brought under state control the most modern, dynamic, and competitive large enterprises in all sectors of economic activity. As Christian Deubner puts it, "It is only due to the extreme dualism of the Portuguese economy that statistically the phenomenon [of state control] appears to be quantitatively produceable to a percentage comparable to other West European states, whereas qualitatively, it may in my opinion not be so compared."[8] The state has moved into all realms of economic activity not only in terms of control, but also direct ownership. Whereas in the Estado Novo the state would legally control economic activity it would do so mainly for the benefit of the trusts. After the revolution the control was made much more direct and would be for the benefit of those deemed worthy, according to new and varying political definitions. For this reason the state itself would be fought over all the more for its increased presence and role in the economy.

Another area of change, and related to the struggle for the state, is the formation of political parties after April 25, 1975. It is worth repeating that parties were not allowed in the old regime and except for the PCP all were formed just before or right after the coup. Obviously there were movement or group bases for these parties, but they were not elaborated, integrated, or tested in political battle. Immediately after April 25 there was a fantastic proliferation of parties—an occurrence which may raise some questions about the implications of corporatism.[9] The variety and number suggests that all groups in the population, regardless of size and ideological orientation, would have a party or movement to represent it. However, as reflected in the elections of 1975 and verified in later elections, only four of these parties (PS, PPD, CDS, and PCP) would receive sufficient votes to be considered viable. Thus in the arena of party politics there would indeed be a substantial change from the old regime, but in relatively normal terms for Western European patterns rather than the hegemony of the PCP or the anarchy of the 50 odd movements of 1974–75.[10]

In the labor system there was initially very little change in structure, but a great deal of change in operation and orientation. In the Estado Novo the corporatist system provided for obligatory and controlled means for the representation of interests, including those of workers. During the few years before 1974 the regime allowed some flexibility; additionally, around this time the Communists founded the Intersindical which operated clandestinely and against the regime. With the coup the union system, ironically enough, was not changed.[11] However, the PCP usurped the entire system of unions, and Intersindical became de facto the only national-level organization for workers. Later, in 1976 there would be some changes in this situation. However, during the revolutionary period the structure of the organization of union control remained largely the same, but with the difference that it was controlled by the revolutionary PCP instead of a conservative corporatist regime.

In moving away from the national level we consider the local level which had, in my view, a more significant level of change. In the revolutionary fervor of 1974–75 the population took matters into its own hands; policies were in a state of flux, the state intervened, and owners and managers departed due to real or imagined fears. This popular involvement took a number of different forms. In neighborhoods, organizations formed and made decisions regarding such issues as education and services. In firms, workers took control in the face of bankruptcy or decapitalization as the owners departed or waited for assurances from the government. These self-help efforts were definitely encouraged by parties such as the MDP/CDE, the MRPP, and even the MFA with its cultural dynaminization campaign. In a firm the result was either the formation of a cooperative or "autogestão," worker self-management. The most reliable statistics indicate that some 220 firms were under worker self-management and another 1,000 were being run as cooperatives. Thus whereas in the old regime the workers had very limited roles in society and industry, in these new forms they had a dominant say in the operations of the firm. However, the most thorough study done to date shows that these efforts at popular participation and control became heavily dependent on the state for financial assistance.[12] Regardless of the viability of these experiences, they were extremely important in allowing popular participation at a local level and giving a certain élan or definition to the revolution process. They proved to be short-lived, but it was encouraging to see the Portuguese so involved and active after such a long time of enforced passivity.

The next and last area of change during the revolutionary period concerns the rural areas. All studies on the agrarian sector in Portugal before the coup give a very negative and bleak impression indeed. This relates not only to the extremely low productivity of the agrarian sector, which even today forces Portugal to massively import agricultural products composing some 20 percent of the country's trade deficit (and this in a low-industrialized agricultural country with 31.5 percent of the population in the primary sector), but to the extremely repressive situation of land tenure. Even as sanitized and noncommital a report as the World Bank study on the agricultural sector dramatizes the tremendous inequalities of wealth and power in the rural areas.[13] This pertains in particular to the southern agricultural region—the Alentejo—as the north is characterized by small family holdings. In the south the holdings were very extensive and land ownership concentrated.[14] Thus for reasons of both efficiency and equality it would have been anticipated that substantial change would occur in the rural area, even if we overlook the control of the PCP in the Alentejo.

As the revolutionary process gathered momentum in late 1974 thereby allowing possibilities for action by workers and peasants, the rural area became the predominant focus of takeovers and violence. Land invasions began in February 1975 and accelerated through May of that year. By the end of 1975 some 480 estates with over 1 million hectares, or 20 percent of the country's agricultural land, was occupied and transformed into collectives or cooperatives. As the World Bank stated, "Within a few months, therefore, the *latifundia* of the Alentejo was virtually abolished and, along with it, the power structure in the rural areas completely altered."[15] After the takeover by the peasants, obviously promoted in most cases by political groups and parties, the government formulated a vast net of agrarian reform legislation which changed as the governments changed. It was not until September 1977 that a major legislative package—the Agrarian Reform Law, 77/77—temporarily clarified and rationalized the situation of land tenure and takeovers. This law was violently opposed by the PCP, and many of those taking over land, and more recently has been opposed for opposite reasons by the Right. Its implementation has proven difficult, and it is likely that the agrarian situation has given rise to more violence than any other single aspect of the revolution with the exception of decolonization. The actions on the land and the politics involved in working out a solution has also been very defining of the Portuguese revolution. The country has gone from an extremely inefficient and unjust system to another which is probably also inefficient but more just. Then, with changes to be discussed in later chapters, there has been a certain rationalization which promises to change the system even more but this time with less popular participation. Moreover, while these takeovers were occurring in the south, with peasant support, they were opposed by peasants in the north who were afraid of losing what little they had.

This is but a summary of some of the major changes brought about in, and by, the revolution and serving to define it. What emerges is the haphazard, anomalous, and even contradictory nature of these changes. Decolonization is a case in itself and, as the empire split from Portugal, is of less interest here except for the influx of refugees and the economic importance of future trade with the excolonies. The changes in political structures such as parties and the union system would continue to change according to the struggle for power. And, the changes in the economy and society would move forward or backward depending on this struggle, in conjunction with Portugal's relationship with foreign powers and institutions. In sum, the revolution is reversible. It was a tremendous leap ahead largely because Portugal was so backward and lacked a regime which was willing (before 1974) or able (after 1974) to define and implement a coherent strategy for modernization.

Notes

1. For a very useful analysis of Portugal and the colonial predicament see Perry Anderson, "Portugal and the End of Ultra-Colonialism," *New Left Review*, vols. 15, 16, 17 (1962).

2. Avelino Rodrigues, et. al., *Portugal Depois de Abril* (Lisbon:Intervoz, 1976), pp. 28, 83–95.

3. On this extremely important topic see, for example, the fol-

lowing: Gerald Bender, "Angola: A Story of Stupidity," *New York Review of Books* 25 (December 21, 1978); Michael Harsgor, "Aftereffects of an 'Exemplary Decolonization'," *Journal of Contemporary History* 15 (1980): 143–67; and F.W. Heimer, *The Decolonization Conflict in Angola, 1974–76* (Geneva: Institut Universitaire de Hautes Etudes Internationales, 1979).

4. For some comparisons between France and Portugal see Douglas Porch, *The Portuguese Armed Forces and the Revolution* (London: Croom Helm, 1977). For a good analysis of other comparisons see Tony Smith, "A Comparative Study of French and British Decolonization," *Comparative Studies in Society and History* 20 (1978): 70–102.

5. See Eric Baklanoff, "The Political Economy of Portugal's Old Regime: Growth and Change Preceding the 1974 Revolution," *World Development* 7 (1979): 799–811. And Francisco Pereira de Moura, *Por Onde Vai a Economia Portuguesa?* 4th ed. (Lisbon: Seara Nova, 1974).

6. Eric Baklanoff, *The Economic Transformation of Spain and Portugal* (New York: Praeger Publishers, 1978), p. 158. The details may be found in M. Belmira Martins and J. Chaves Rosa, *O Grupo Estado* (Lisbon: Edições Expresso, 1979).

7. On the processes of takeover see for example Phil Mailer, *Portugal: The Impossible Revolution?* (London: Solidarity, 1977) and Maria de Lurdes Lima Santos, et al., *O 25 de Abril e as Lutas Sociais nas Empresas* (Porto: Afrontamento, 1976) in two volumes.

8. A mimeographed document, 1979. See his "Die Europaische Gemeinschaft und Portugal: Zu einigen Hauptfragen des portugiesischen Beitritts zur EG," Stiftung Wissenschaft und Politik, Ebenhausen, September 1980. For a listing of the nationalizations and a discussion of their importance in the economy see Martins, Rosa, *O Grupo Estado*.

9. Philippe Schmitter raises some of these questions at the end of his *Corporatism and Public Policy in Authoritarian Portugal*, Contemporary Political Sociology Series, vol. 1 (Beverly Hills: Sage Publications, 1975).

10. Juan J. Linz provides a comparative perspective on this question in his "Europe's Southern Frontier: Evolving Trends Toward What?," *Deadalus* (Winter, 1979): 175–209.

11. On the system in the old regime see, for example, Mário Pinto and Carlos Moura, *As Estruturas Sindicais Portuguesas: Contributo para o Seu Estudo* (Lisbon: Gabinete de Investigações Sociais, 1973). My interviews provided the details since the revolution.

12. See Nancy Bermeo, "Worker Management in Industry: Reconciling Representative Government in a Polarized Society," in *In Search of Modern Portugal*, eds. Lawrence Graham and Douglas Wheeler (Madison: University of Wisconsin Press, 1983), pp. 181–98.

See, as well, Mailer, *Portugal: The Impossible Revolution?* and dos Santos, *O 25 de Abril.* The journal *Análise Social* provides a good deal of analysis on this topic.

13. The World Bank, *Portugal: Agricultural Sector Survey* (Washington: The World Bank, November 1978).

14. *Portugal Information,* February 1976, p. 16.

15. The World Bank, 1978, p. 13. There is a decent amount of material on the topic of agricultural structures and agrarian reform. See the following simply as examples of this material: Antonio Barreto, *Pour une Réforme Agraire Démocratique et Constitutionnelle* (Lisbon: n.p., 1977); Earl O. Heady, *Análise do Desenvolvimento Agrícola e da Reforma Agrária em Portugal* (Lisbon: MAP, December 1977); J. Carvalho Cardoso, *A Agricultura Portuguesa* (Lisbon: Moraes Editores, 1973); João Garin, *Reforma Agrária: Seara de Odio* (Lisbon: Edições do Templo, 1977); and Gonçalo Santa-Ritta, *Portugal: Agricultura e Problemas Humanos* (Lisbon: Terra Livre, 1979). The newest publication is Michel Drain and Bernard Domenach, *Occupations de Terres et Expropriations dans les Campagnes Portugaises* (Paris: Editions du CNRS, 1982). A new series under the editorship of Antonio Barreto has begun to be published in Portugal in early 1983.

4

From the MFA Revolution to November 25, 1975, and the FAP (Portuguese Armed Forces)

The period and the material covered in this chapter are important for they concern Portugal's move from a radical and predominantly military government to a model found mainly in Europe and North America: that is, a liberal democratic regime. Usually when a conservative authoritarian regime is overthrown from the Left there is either a consolidation of power by the Left or, in reaction, a military dictatorship from the Right. In Portugal, however, the process of radicalization in 1974–75, and the reaction to it, culminated in the removal of the military from power and the establishment of a civilian regime. This chapter will analyze how the political parties (and not just the PCP as was the case during the previous year) succeeded in defining their role in the political system. This is in direct contrast as well to the latter half of 1974 when the parties were somewhat marginalized and the MFA, with support of the PCP, was seeking institutionalization. As we shall see, the evolution of the Portuguese situation was due not only to the interaction of parties, the military, and social forces in Portugal, but the direct and indirect involvement of a variety of foreign states and organizations.

The political-military crisis of the summer of 1975 began to be resolved in August when the Nine in the Revolutionary Council issued their Document, galvanizing military and civilian elements into opposition to Premier Vasco Gonçalves. During the summer of 1975 there was no single political regime in Portugal but rather a number of competing ones that were promoted by groups with changing levels of power. Premier Vasco Gonçalves, with the support of the PCP, advocated a regime which looked increasingly like an orthodox Communist model.[1] The MFA Assembly seemed captivated by a model based on "popular power" in which the link between the people and the revolutionary military would be direct. In the Document of the Nine the moderates emphasized the transition to socialism, but through a pluralistic approach. In reaction to these options, a document published on August 13 by the military intervention force, COPCON, argued frantically for the "popular power" model. And finally there was the PS and parties to its Right which stood for a liberal democratic model.[2] With the removal of Premier Vasco Gonçalves in early September, the only model which was apparently eliminated for reasons of domestic opposition and international unacceptability was the one he and the PCP were promoting. All of the other competing models remained, and in the intervening struggle for power one after another was eliminated until, in 1976, one would be implemented.

The removal of Premier Vasco Gonçalves necessitated the formation of yet another provisional government, the sixth since April 25, 1974. During this period of late summer and fall 1975 if any group could be said to have power it was the Revolutionary Council, which in early September reinstated Major Melo Antunes and Commander Vitor Alves, both of whom had been forced out by Gonçalvist elements after the Document of the Nine. The Revolutionary Council, in conjunction with the main political parties, required three weeks to form the Sixth Provisional Government which finally took office on September 19. It was difficult to form this government because of the lack of agreement over the type of regime and the fragmentation of groups seeking power. Finally, however, the composition reflected the actual configuration of forces in the military and the results of the elections to the Constituent Assembly. There were five military moderates, the premier was Commander Pinheiro de Azevedo, there were four members of the PS, two of the PPD, and one of the PCP. In no case was the leader of a party in the government, as everyone realized in advance that this government faced a difficult prospect and was likely to be unpopular. After more than a year of politicization and revolutionary activity, nobody had any illusions about the power of a government to rule.

Most seriously, it was an open question whether the military retained sufficient coherence to avoid civil war—let alone provide support and legitimacy to the government. The purges and politicization of the previous year had taken their toll: symptomatic of the overall military situation was the military intervention force, COPCON. In reaction to General Spínola's support within the military hierarchy, this force was created in July of 1974 and Otelo Saraiva de Carvalho promoted from Captain to Brigadier General to head it as well as the Lisbon Military Region. The intervention force was to control disruption and violence which the police, now lacking the secret police and with the GNR very weak, were unable to deal with. However, Otelo himself became extremely politicized and, like many other members of COPCON, very much taken with his own importance. It was penetrated by such radical groups as the MRPP and the PRP-BR. Thus rather than serving as an intervention force to maintain order it supported demonstrations, takeovers, and popular movements, and the military elements under its supposed control joined—instead of constraining—political and social movements. As Otelo stated it, "the workers are in the right unless it is proven otherwise."[3] If this elite unit was part of the revolution, then what support could the Nine in the Revolutionary Council count on? They predominated at the political level but within every batallion, unit, and barracks there remained a variety of factions with different political orientations. There remained as well a whole panoply of service or support units which had as their main function the political mobilization of the military.[4] The government could not, therefore, rely on the units and neither they, nor anyone else, controlled the overall military situation. The president since General Spínola's resignation in September 1974 was General Costa Gomes. His role was particularly ambiguous in this period, but it is clear that he did not control either the political or military situation. It was intentional that he was called "the cork," for he displayed an uncanny ability to bob up and down with the political tide.[5]

The Sixth Provisional Government was the first government since the collapse the previous September of the Second Provisional Government due to General Spínola's resignation, which was not overtly and aggressively revolutionary. Further, it would necessarily be somewhat conservative against the tide of movements and demonstrations and in the context of an increasingly severe economic situation as reserves of foreign exchange ran low. Its tasks, therefore, were tremendous but it lacked the instruments to deal with them. The revolutionary momentum and aspirations continued, fanned by a broad variety of parties and movements of the Left. The public administration was not particularly strong before 1974 and after the coup was usurped by competing political parties and groups which cancelled one another and thereby paralyzed the bureaucracy. And, additionally, many civil servants who were identified with the old regime were forced out, thereby decreasing the degree of experience and competence within the administration.[6] Moreover, the higher levels of the military were ambiguous. When the Sixth Provisional Government took office the Chief of Staff of the Army, General Fabião, and Otelo as head of COPCON and the Lisbon military region, declared their support. After the Government had been in office but a short time, Otelo announced that his support was conditional and by the end of September he confirmed his opposition to the Government. As his units would be the ones to support the Government, this made governing very tricky indeed. General Fabião proved to be even weaker and more ambiguous than President Costa Gomes. He was indecisive, contradictory, and even assisted at a revolutionary swearing-in ceremony in the military.[7]

With this background it is no surprise that the period between mid-September and late November was extremely chaotic. There were massive strikes and demonstrations, disruption, political posturing and threats, and the formation of revolutionary cells—the SUVs—within the military. Some of the more notable events include the following: the disappearance of a thousand automatic rifles which were passed to civilians by military radicals; the refusal by units in the military police to board ship to Angola where they would supervise the decolonization process; the imprisonment of the Premier and the members of the Constituent Assembly in São Bento Palace by thousands of protesting workers between November 12 and 14; and the Government's response of going on strike on November 18 until they received full support from the Revolutionary Council to govern. Even before this, on November 7, the Revolutionary Council ordered the dynamiting of the Church's radio station, Radio Renasçenca, which had been taken over by the far Left. These were incredible times, surrealistic and unbelievable, but fraught with real danger because of the factions and splits within the military and the arming of civilians. In short, Portugal was in a state of anarchy.[8]

The Nine of the Revolutionary Council and their cohorts realized this situation could not continue. Already in late Sep-

tember they asked Lieutenant Colonel Ramalho Eanes to develop a plan of operations in case they had to move militarily.[9]
And, with the imprisonment of the Government on November
12 and a victory celebration planned by the Left for November
16, the Nine met with their allies on November 15 to prepare
for any eventuality.[10] Of the political parties at least the PS was
aware of the plans, but apparently not directly involved at this
point. There was a widespread feeling that the first group to
move, Left-Right-whatever, was likely to be smashed. Preparation was made on all sides for a military, or at least armed
action, but from the sources available it would appear that the
Nine and their allies did not initiate what came to be the
aborted coup of November 25. It is probably as accurate to say
that the PCP brought on March 11, as it is to say that the Nine
instigated November 25. Obviously there were complicated interactions, but the situation is comprehensible.[11] If any single
action on their part brought on the attempted coup it was the
nomination of one of their members, and an original member
along with Otelo of the MFA, Vasco Lourenço, as commander
of the Lisbon Military Region. Otelo would become Vice Chief
of the General Staff and COPCON would be abolished. Clearly
this was an attempt to consolidate their power, and the Nine
were opposed by those seeking to maintain the revolutionary
line. As usual President Costa Gomes equivocated, but the
Nine persisted. At the same time, on November 24, at Rio
Maior members of the CAP (Confederation of Portuguese Ag-
riculturalists) halted all rail and road traffic between Lisbon
and the Northern part of the country. This meant that Lisbon
would be isolated in the event of civil war and demonstrated as
well the increasingly strong feelings of some civilian groups.
There is evidence that political parties were indeed involved,
but even so it appears that this action had wide popular support.[12]

In the early morning of November 25 Leftist units, beginning with the paratroopers at Tancos, moved to take over the
centers of military power. They initially had the advantage,
but in the face of the preparation of Ramalho Eanes and Jaime
Neves they were quickly outmaneuvered and defeated by the
following day. The attempted coup showed that the Left in the
military was poorly organized, ill-prepared, and had suffered
from the politicization of the previous year. None of the Leftist
units around Lisbon were able to put up much of a battle and
the fighting proved that the Nine did in fact control a military

apparatus which worked.[13] November 25 also demonstrated
that the PCP was not adventuristic in that they quickly saw
that the military Left would not win and thus completely and
totally disassociated themselves from it. Additionally, popular
support fared no better for the civilians who had been armed
were extremely disorganized and no more competent than the
military Left. The success of the Nine and their allies was total. They then purged the Revolutionary Council of Otelo Fabião, and Admiral Rosa Coutinho as a prelude to purging the
Left in the military.[14] Thus the Nine, beginning to advance in
the summer of 1975, took control of the military after November 25 while the forces of the Left in general, and in the military in particular, backed off.

The success of the Nine and their allies allowed for the definition of a new regime. After November 25 all of the competing models of regime previously mentioned, save that of the
Nine and the parties, became impossible. Vasco Gonçalves was
out and the PCP weakened; the proponents of popular power
had been defeated and the COPCON was eliminated. November 25 was a watershed second in importance only to April 25,
1975. Now, however, the main preoccupation was the rise of
the Right rather than the rise of the Left. It is important that a
key figure throughout this period was Major Melo Antunes.
He had written all of the key documents from the original Program to the Document of the Nine and was directly involved in
the preparations for November 25.[15] He went on television on
November 26 and defended the PCP against efforts to outlaw
it. The significance of this intervention was to allow the PCP to
serve as a counterweight to the increasing strength of the
Right; of course, in a liberal democratic system parties, unless
they are violent, are allowed to operate. By this time the PCP
was a good deal more circumscribed in its statements and actions. Melo Antunes was closely involved with Lieutenant
Colonel Ramalho Eanes; the two held similar positions on
most important issues, except the former preferred a greater
ongoing role for the remnants of the MFA in preventing a drift
to the Right. He of course realized that the role of the military
would have to be more restricted, defined, and limited so that
the regime could incorporate the political parties as key actors. The difficulty was, of course, that it would be very touchy
for the remnants of the MFA to supervise while the parties presumably governed.

The actual implementation would be done more by Ra-malho Eanes than Melo Antunes. After leading the military movement against the coup of November 25, he became Chief of Staff on December 5. From the first moment he defined his task as making the army into an apolitical force at the service of the whole country.[16] In his plans the armed forces would be reorganized in such a way that the MFA was superseded; this would eliminate the possibility of the MFA once again occupy-ing the center of the political stage effectively. In this way the system could evolve in a civilian direction.[17] In Eanes's plans for reorganization not only would the specific functions of the armed forces be defined, but their size would be cut as well from the approximately 200,000 to about 75,000 two years later. Clearly, then, with the changes after November 25 and particularly with the individuals who came out on top, the mili-tary was to be much restricted in its role.

This period in late 1975 was very important and foreign states and institutions were heavily involved. In particular, the United States and the Federal Republic of Germany showed their support for the Sixth Provisional Government af-ter November 25 by agreeing to a number of loans and grants for a variety of projects. In effect, they showed their willing-ness to commit themselves to this Government which was evolving toward increased civilian control.[18] The Socialist In-ternational was extremely active in providing support for the PS, encouraging the EEC to provide loans, and providing moral support through such events as the meeting of the So-cialist International in Oporto in March 1976. The effort was to build up the PS as a party and to link Portugal with Western Europe. At this period, however, probably the most important international effort involved the military and NATO. In his plans for reorganization of the military Eanes was in close con-tact with the Americans, Germans, and other NATO allies. The American army attaché went with Eanes to NATO in February 1976, and there were other exchanges both to and from Portu-gal. The reorganization came to include the formation of a Por-tuguese brigade for use on the southern flank of NATO. This brigade was to be trained and equipped by NATO allies and was the most obvious manifestation (as the U.S. ambassador had his picture taken in one of the tanks for this brigade) of a much broader plan of cooperation which would include credits and grants for a panoply of military equipment. In sum, with the military and then increasingly political definition after November 25, Western European and North American political actors became more deeply involved in linking the country to them and providing support so that the strain would not be too great for democratic Portugal. Thus after late 1975 as the system became increasingly sorted out, most of the inputs would be from Western countries seeking to integrate Portugal into a similar kind of political system.

The Party Pact of April 11, 1975, which registered the configuration of forces in that period of revolutionary fervor, was no longer appropriate in changed circumstances. With the MFA effectively disbanded it could no longer serve as the vanguard of a revolution which appeared to have reached its end; what is more, the political parties, except for the PCP, were not enthusiastic about a Pact in which they were marginalized. Thus after November 25 there was a general sense that the Pact had to be revised. The officers initially suggested the idea, but the exact nature of the new pact would take some two months to work out in negotiations between Melo Antunes and other members of the Revolutionary Council and the main parties. The resulting Pact—Armed Forces-Political Parties—of February 26, 1976, stipulated that the Revolutionary Council would not be disbanded, but continue less as a vanguard and more as a guarantor of the revolution. In military terms it would maintain a large role, but politically its most important function would be to advise the president who would chair the Council. In addition, a Constitutional Commission was provided for in the Revolutionary Council to judge on the constitutionality of law. The Pact, in fact, set forth a general statement on the regime then in formation and would later be incorporated in the Constitution. The details of the Pact, as well as the fact that it required two months of negotiations rather than the hurried imposition of the first Pact, demonstrated that the coalition of forces in Portugal had changed substantially.[19] As part of the understanding of the Pact and its inclusion in the Constitution was the stipulation that this latter document could not be changed during the first legislature. The Council, then, would continue for at least four years. This would be one of the continuations of the MFA, now embodied in the Council, which included many of the founders of the movement in what was likely going to be a civilian government.

Probably just as important for the continuation of the Council was an understanding that the president would be a military man, presumably linked to the Nine.[20] This was not stipulated in the Pact, but rather concerned whom the parties would support as their candidate. As General Eanes had shown himself to be not only an extremely competent commander and Chief of Staff but also in favor of a civilian regime, he was the logical candidate. However, Eanes was not originally interested in the position and it took some convincing by Melo Antunes to persuade him to run.[21] He was quickly supported by the three major parties, excluding the PCP which ran their own candidate, and indeed carried 62 percent of the vote in the June election. His opponents included the PCP's Octavio Pato, Otelo Saraiva de Carvalho, and Pinheiro de Azevedo. None of these were viable candidates as the election results showed: Otelo had 16 percent, Azevedo 14 percent, and Pato 8 percent. Thus the president for the next four years was a general who supported the MFA, became involved with the Nine, put down the attempted coup from the Left, and reorganized the armed forces. This background, with a large percentage of the popular vote put him in a very strong position indeed.

The same could not be said of the government resulting from the elections to the Assembly of the Republic on April 25, 1976. The results were similar to those to the Constituent Assembly a year before and gave the PS 35 percent, PPD 24 percent, CDS 16 percent, and PCP 14 percent. Clearly, then, no single party stood out despite the role of the PS in opposing the PCP and the extensive international support the PS received. The implications of this will be dealt with in the next chapter.

The Constitution which defines the presidency and the Assembly of the Republic was promulgated on April 2, 1976. It is a document many thought would never be implemented for it was written during a period when revolutionary activity was threatening to make the Constituent Assembly irrelevant. This is not the place to go into details (it will be discussed in Chapter Seven), but it is necessary to point out that the Constitution represented the mood and configuration of forces in 1975 and early 1976 in which the PS and the PCP struggled for ascendancy, while the main parties to the Right, the PPD and the CDS, were very much on the defensive. The Constitution is extremely advanced in goals, extensive in details, and comprehensive in scope. With 312 items it is reputedly the third longest in the world. It was approved by the representatives of all the parties but the CDS and provides for "assuring the transition to socialism through the creation of conditions for the democratic exercise of power by the working classes" and states "the development of the revolutionary process imposes, on the economic plane, the collective appropriation of the principal means of production."[22] It is most definitely not a statement in favor of laissez-faire capitalism as it guarantees a whole series of rights to the workers. It stipulated that its amendment was prohibited during the first legislature and after that only by a two-thirds vote of the Assembly.

By late summer 1976 the political situation was very different from what it had been a year earlier during the "Hot Summer of 1975." The military had now been reorganized and increasingly depoliticized while the links with NATO were expanded; there was a popularly elected president who originated in the Nine and was advised by a Revolutionary Council composed of original MFA elements; the elections of April 25, 1976, produced a government which was composed of much the same elements as that of a year earlier; and there was a very comprehensive and advanced constitution which guaranteed and enshrined many of the most important gains from the revolution.

What was the role of international factors in this evolution, not to say domestication, of the Portuguese revolution? The USSR was not willing to support the PCP in what appeared to be a leap for power. The PCP was the only serious contender for power on the Left as the other groups and movements would either self-destruct in internecine ideological battles or cancel one another out. The PCP maintained its coherence and ideological definition and did in fact achieve a great deal of influence. However, it could not have taken power on its own without support from the USSR and this was not forthcoming. Rather, the USSR provided ongoing encouragement, but backed down in extreme activities such as actually assuming power and seeking to influence events through the MFA. There was too much at stake. The West made it very evident that Portugal was an integral part of Western Europe and thus not open to Soviet adventurism. President Ford made this clear as did Secretary of State Kissinger, and there were conversations as well between Willy Brandt and Secretary Brezhnev. At both the public and private levels, it was certain the NATO countries would not allow Portugal to be ruled by the PCP.[23]

Defeat of the PCP was one thing and establishment of a liberal democratic regime another. A more likely scenario would have been anarchy during the fall of 1975 followed by a Rightist military coup. Here we must remind ourselves once again that the elements who won on November 25 were those who formulated the original Program of the MFA and who consistently advocated a civilian regime, albeit a progressive one. To these observations, however, must be included the very important integration with NATO which gave the military a professional purpose, as well as support, and it is no secret that the NATO allies told the Portuguese that a coup would not be tolerated.[24] An additional factor in averting a takeover from the Right (or either side) was economic support: for the country as a whole, and for the parties—particularly the PS. These supports came in many forms for many purposes and share only the fact that they allowed the country to avoid polarization despite the influx of more than a half million refugees, the exhaustion of the foreign exchange reserves, and the difficulty of sorting out the economic system after takeovers and nationalizations. The support included development projects, food aid, refugee aid, balance of payments supports, and loans for the purchase of a variety of goods.[25] Undoubtedly this assistance was important in allowing leeway in post-revolutionary Portugal and in linking the country with other liberal democratic regimes.

In late summer 1976 Portugal was a functioning liberal democratic regime which had just emerged from two years of decolonization and revolutionary activity. It was a regime which inherited the legacy of these rapid processes but not a legacy of functioning democracy. It could, however, rely on external support. It was in this context that the PS of Mario Soares formed a government based only on the PS with 107 deputies in an Assembly of 263 members (PDP:73, CDS:42, PCP:40) and began to govern within the guidelines of the Constitution.

Notes

1. It is useful to review Gonçalves' speeches to have a sense of how he had evolved from mid-1974 to the spring of 1975. See, for example, Vasco Gonçalves, *Discursos, Conferencias de Imprensa, En-*

trevistas (Porto: Edição Popular, 1976) and for an attempt to analyze these speeches see Rui de Brito, *Anatomia das Palavras* (Lisbon: Liber, 1976).

2. Most of the documentation can be found in the appendixes of Avelino Rodrigues, et al., *O Movimento dos Capitães e o 25 de Abril* (Lisbon: Moraes Editores, 1974); idem, *Portugal Depois de Abril* (Lisbon: Intervoz, 1976); idem, *Abril nos Quartéis de Novembêro* (Lisbon: Livraria Bertrand, 1979).

3. On Otelo Saraiva de Carvalho see not only his *Cinco Meses Mudaram Portugal* (Lisbon: Portugália Editora, 1975) and *Alvorada em Abril* (Amadora: Livraria Bertrand, 1977), but also António Tavares-Teles, *Otelo* (Lisbon: 18 de Janeiro editora, 1976), and Jean Pierre Faye, ed. *Portugal: The Revolution in the Labyrinth* (London: Spokesman Books, 1976) which is drawn from papers of the Russell Committee for Portugal and mainly about Otelo. For more critical comments on Otelo see José Gomes Mota, *A Resistência: O Verão Quente de 1975* (Lisbon: Edicões Expresso, 1976).

4. Avelino Rodrigues, et al., *Abril nos Quartéis de Novembêro* (Lisbon: Livraria Bertrand, 1979), pp. 170–71.

5. For President Costa Gomes's speeches see his *Discursos Politicos* (Lisbon: Ministério da Comunicação Social, 1976).

6. See Lawrence S. Graham, "Bureaucratic Politics and the Problem of Reform in the State Apparatus," in *In Search of Modern Portugal: The Revolution and Its Consequences*, eds. Lawrence S. Graham and Douglas Wheeler (Madison: University of Wisconsin Press, 1983), pp. 223–50.

7. José Gomes Mota, *A Resistência* (Lisbon: Edicões Expresso, 1976), pp. 139–43, provides critical comments on Fabião.

8. A very good sense of the mood in Portugal at that time is provided by Jane Kramer's "A Reporter at Large: The Portuguese Revolution," *The New Yorker*, December 15, 1975, pp. 92–133.

9. Rodrigues, *Portugal Depois de Abril*, p. 258; idem, *Abril nos Quartéis de Novembêro* (Lisbon: Livraria Bertrand, 1979), pp. 128–29.

10. Mota, *A Resistência*, pp. 179–80.

11. Rodrigues, *Abril nos Quartéis de Novembêro*, p. 151. There is much material on the attempted coup of November 25. For a view favorable to Otelo see Faye, *Portugal: The Revolution in the Labyrinth*. For two books favorable to those who won in the events see L. Pereira Gil, *Novembêro 25: Anatomia de um Golpe* (Lisbon: Edição Editus, 1976) and Freire Antunes, *O Segredo do 25 de Novembêro* (Lisbon: Europe-America, 1980). There is also a two volume official report entitled *Relatório do 25 de Novembêro de 1975* (Texto Integral) (Lisbon: Ed. Abril, 1976). And, for a book by one who lost on November 25, see Manual Duran Clemente, *Elementos para a compreensão do 25 de Novembêro* (Lisbon: Edições Sociais, 1976).

12. Mota, *A Resistência*, p. 188, on the party's involvement.

13. See Gil, *Novembro 25*; Antunes, *O Segredo do 25 de Novembêro*; *Relatório do 25 de Novembêro*. See also Douglas Porch, *The Portuguese Armed Forces and the Revolution* (London: Croom Helm, 1977), pp. 222–38.

14. Extensive details on the purges, in comparison with earlier purges from the Left are found in Rodrigues, *Abril nos Quartéis de Novembêro*.

15. A particularly useful interview with Melo Antunes can be found in *Cadernos de O Jornal: Os Herdeiros do 25 de Abril* (Lisbon: O Jornal, April 1976), pp. 84–98.

16. See the commentary in Rodrigues, *Abril nos Quartéis de Novembêro*, p. 161. There is also a very good analysis on reorganization of the armed forces by Marcelo Rebelo de Sousa in *Expresso*, 13 December 1975.

17. Rodrigues, *Abril nos Quartéis de Novembêro*, pp. 176–77 deal with the "death" of the MFA. For information on the discussion over this issue see U.S. Congress, Senate, Committee on Foreign Relations, *Revolution into Democracy: Portugal after the Coup* prepared by Senator George McGovern. August 1976, p. 56.

18. This point was emphasized in particular by officials in the American and German embassies in Lisbon. For details see note 23.

19. The Pact was published as *Plataforma de Acordo Constitucional Entre o MFA e Os Partidos Políticos* (Lisbon: Ministério da Communicação Social, February 1976). An extremely useful analysis of the contrast between the first and second Pacts, and the negotiations involved, is found in *Expresso*, 28 February 1976.

20. Robert Harvey, *Portugal: Birth of a Democracy* (London: Macmillan Press, 1978), p. 106. McGovern, "Revolution into Democracy," p. 59.

21. Interviews in Lisbon. Still the most useful book on General Eanes is Paulino Gomes and Tomás C. Bruneau, *Eanes: Porque o Poder?* (Lisbon: Intervoz, 1976). In collaborating on this book I learned a great deal about the president and Melo Antunes from journalists who knew them well. I have also interviewed Major Melo Antunes.

22. For incredible details on the Constitution see either Jorge Miranda, *Constituição e Democracia* (Lisbon: Livraria Petrony, 1976) or Reinaldo Caldeira and Maria do Céu Silva, *Constituição Política da República Portuguesa, 1976* (Lisbon: Livraria Bertrand, 1976). Both of these include positions of the parties, debates, and comparisons. For a more general comparative analysis see Marcelo Rebelo de Sousa, *Direito Constitucional* (Braga: Livraria Cruz, 1979).

23. See McGovern, "Revolution into Democracy," pp. 76–81. I also found useful the section on Portugal in *Report on West European Communist Parties*, submitted by Senator Edward W. Brooke to the Committee on Appropriations, United States Senate, June 1977, pp.

113–37. And, of considerable use, is the chapter entitled "Portugal and Southern Africa: Setback and Rebound," in *The Diplomacy of Detente: The Kissinger Era,* Coral Bell (N.Y.: St. Martin's Press, 1977), pp. 156–83.

24. This point is based on interviews in Washington, D.C., and with the embassies in Lisbon. Most of these interviews were conducted in 1976 and 1977.

25. An incomplete list of foreign assistance to Portugal between 1975 and 1981 is as follows:

European Economic Community (1 ecu = $1.3).

180 million, October 1975 Special emergency financial aid.

200 million, July 1976 Financial protocol to 1972 free trade agreement.

Smaller sums (100,000 and 300,000) for flood and earthquake victims.

275 million, May 1981 for preaccession assistance.

(Sources: Europe Information, 34/80 and Press releases)

Federal Republic of Germany

DM 420 million, 95% Government guarantee for West German private banks' credit to Banco do Portugal.

$75 and $250 million, 1976, from Federal Bank of West Germany to Banco do Portugal, balance of payments support.

DM 530 million, until 1979, for development projects.

DM 25 million, until 1979, for technical cooperation.

ca DM 42 million, until 1979, for unspecified purposes from foundations.

(Sources: Informed German sources and interviews at German Embassy, Lisbon)

United States

$215 million, 1976–81 for grains under PL 480.

$590 million, 1976–80, CCC for grains, cotton, etc.

$300 milllion, 1977 for balance of payments support.

$182 million, by 1979, for development projects.

(Sources: *Expresso,* 14 March 1981; interviews in Washington and Embassy in Lisbon)

World Bank

$518 million, 1976–80 for development projects.

(Source: *Expresso,* 7 March 1980).

These figures do not include the $750 million consortium, requiring IMF initial approval for $50 million, which was put together by United States $300 million, Germany $200 million, Japan $50 million, Venezuela $22.5 million, etc.

Nor do they include military assistance that seems to average about $30 million per year from the United States, probably about half this from Germany, and lesser sums from other NATO allies.

There are in addition payments, or lease agreements with the Americans for Lajes in Azores, Beja with the Germans, and the French for Flores in the Azores.

These are in addition to undetermined sums from a variety of foundations and institutions.

Another listing and subsequent analysis of much but not all of the assistance is Abel Moreira Mateus, "Crescimento Económico e Dívida Externa: O Caso de Portugal" (Lisbon: Instituto de Estudos para o Desenvolvimento, Caderno 5, 1982).

5

Politics in the
Liberal Democratic Regime:
Constitutional Governments I–VI

In the summer of 1976 Portugal installed the first popularly elected government in fifty years. The overall charter was the Constitution which came into force on April 25, 1976, after having been approved by the parties in the Constituent Assembly with the exception of the 16 deputies of the CDS. The government was formed according to the results of the elections to the Assembly of the Republic on April 25, 1976, which saw a voter turnout of 86 percent. The president was elected on June 27 with a 75 percent voter turnout. On July 23 the first constitutional government was sworn in, thus completing a process begun slightly more than two years earlier. A system was now in place which allowed representation for the majority of the Portuguese population and would have to deal with the realities of the country: unresolved problems that had led to the coup in the first place as well as tensions resulting from the subsequent years of revolutionary activity.

Before studying the politics under the Constitution of 1976, it is necessary to at least briefly review some of the types of issues and problems the government would have to confront. Of fundamental importance was the fact that Portugal no longer held a colonial empire, but had instead shrunk to a mere 5 percent of its former territory. The implications arising from this fact are several: The identity of the country from at least the fifteenth century had been defined as an Atlantic and colonial vocation and indeed this was a central element in the propaganda of the Estado Novo. Thus the Portuguese have come to terms with the fact they they could no longer even pretend to be a great power—holding the third largest colonial em-

pire during the era of colonialism—but had to recognize that
they were indeed a very small country and a poor one at that.[1]
Further, while colonialism did not necessarily enrich Portugal, decolonization could well lead to increased impoverish-
ment with the loss of protected markets and cheap sources of
raw materials. To the ideological dimension, then, was added
the very substantial one of loss of resources.

The issue of decolonization had led to the coup which subsequently became a revolution. The old regime was disintegrating and the socioeconomic system it secured so archaic
that revolution easily dismantled much of what had existed before 1974. However, there had been no coherent strategy or
model and thus the polity, economy, and society remained dis-
rupted, unintegrated, and generally confused. The new government would be obliged to put together the pieces of a new
system and integrate them. This "rationalization" would have
to be done by any government, but what was sadly lacking in
post-coup Portugal was a public administration that might
serve as an efficient tool of government. The administration in
the old regime had been fashioned to exploit the colonies and
control the population at home, while providing minimal service. During the revolutionary period this administration was
politicized, and thus the administration itself would have to be
reformulated as the larger system was rationalized.

This rationalization would be the stuff of politics under the
constitutional government(s). Portugal in the summer of 1976
might best be viewed as a number of options, rather than a particular socioeconomic system. The political system, in general
terms, had become liberal democratic. There were so many
haphazard, even contradictory, socioeconomic changes, however, that elements were present for any variety of systems. It
would be the task of politics to gather up the common elements, fashion a system, and seek to integrate it into some
kind of coherent whole. It seemed unlikely that the system
could become more socialized or nationalized, and most likely
there would be a certain regression to some elements of the old
regime once those groups which had been marginalized during the revolution reorganized and gained strength. This is
what politics would be about in the constitutional system.

Yet the developments in Portugal would have to be influenced by external conditions. Most obvious was the serious

economic situation. As the World Bank stated in the first section of the 1978 study on the Portuguese economy: "In terms of the world economy and its impact on a domestic situation, the Portuguese revolution could not have found a time more likely to complicate the adjustment and impede future growth than April 1974."[2] The oil price increase substantially worsened the country's terms of trade, the downturn in Western Europe slackened the demand for the country's exports and decreased the earnings from tourism and the demand for Portuguese workers. The decreased demand for workers was further exacerbated by the return of approximately half a million people from the excolonies. As banks, insurance companies, industries, and businesses were nationalized, investment stopped and trained technicians and managers left the country. Capital inflows from tourism and emigrants' remittances dropped off, and thus the country was unable to balance the trade accounts as had been the case before 1974. Thus export receipts (both goods and nonfactor services such as tourism earnings) fell by about 30 percent in real terms between 1973 and 1975. As a consequence, the current account surplus of $350 million in 1973 become an $820 million deficit in 1975 and increased to some $1.5 billion in 1977. This was all the more serious for "It should be noted that it was the decline in exports and the terms of trade loss which produced this effect, rather than any sharp increase in imports which were only 6 percent above the 1973 level in real terms by 1977. Sustaining deficits of this magnitude has meant a depletion of Portugal's previously ample foreign reserves, and substantial borrowing against its gold reserves."[3] The full implications of the constraints arising from the serious economic situation are highlighted by the fact that Portugal had to turn to the International Monetary Fund for exceptional support in the second half of 1977. A country does not turn to the Fund unless there are severe disequilibria, and once a letter of intent is signed the government is constrained in a number of important areas of economic policy making.[4]

Yet external conditions did not completely determine developments in Portugal. If, on the one hand, there were the severe economic constraints, on the other there were political commitments by states and institutions to support Portuguese democracy. Portugal's case did not resemble Chile's, for example, where important international actors conspired to pressure the government of Salvador Allende. Rather, most of the actors were committed for strategic and other reasons to support the Portuguese experiment in democracy as the country is part of NATO, a likely member of the EEC, and an example of how a Rightist regime was overthown and replaced not by a Leftist regime or a dictatorship but a liberal democratic government. In short, the international constraints would be qualified to a substantial degree by political commitments which provided economic and other support for Portugal.

Thus the summer of 1976 saw a liberal democratic regime in place with a popularly elected government; admittedly it was faced with a number of very difficult problems, but this was somewhat compensated by a degree of electoral legitimacy and external support. The Constitution of 1976 which provided the general orientation for the system can give some insights into what kind of system the Portuguese had defined for themselves. According to one of the most respected constitutional experts, Dr. Jorge Miranda, there are five main themes in the Constitution. (1) National Independence, which is dealt with in at least 12 articles and defines the independence of the Portuguese in political, social, economic, and cultural terms. (2) Fundamental Rights and Liberties, which are dealt with in at least three articles and have no parallel in the constitutions of other countries. They include an extensive series of guarantees and indicate that all the fundamental rights must be interpreted in harmony with the Universal Declaration of Human Rights. (3) Political Democracy, which is dealt with in at least 23 articles, specifies the liberal democratic regime in terms of ideological and partisan pluralism. It stipulates that there will be universal suffrage, separation of powers, and a central role for political parties. What is more the stipulations apply not only to the national but also the regional and local level and even to trade unions. (4) The State of Law is dealt with in at least five articles. It concerns the protection of fundamental rights and restrictions by the government over the people. (5) The Transition to Socialism is dealt with in at least ten articles and stipulates that Portugal is to move democratically toward a socialist economic system. This is not only an abstract guarantee, but includes specific and concrete items such as rights of workers, the role of worker's commissions, unions, and the situation of nationalizations. It must be emphasized that the movement toward socialism is viewed in the Constitution as part and parcel of the process of democratization in Portugal.[5] The Constitution, then, incorporated a particular approach to modernization which included not only the widest and deepest aspects of liberal democracy, but also the consolidation of the socioeconomic changes arising from the revolution which approximate a socialist socioeconomic system. It must be reiterated that the Constitution, although formally opposed only by the CDS, represented the orientation of the PCP and PS and in particular the period in which the members of the Constituent Assembly were elected and the document written. That is to say it was produced during a period of revolution when it seemed likely that the Constitution would be superseded by a more revolutionary statement.

In the elections to the Assembly of the Republic, the PS won more votes than any other party but by no means a majority. Still, with 107 deputies, or approximately 40 percent of the total, the PS of Mario Soares decided to form a government. This was done despite the need for support in the Assembly to pass legislation and ultimately to remain in office. An alliance with the PCP was rejected for reasons of international concern and because much of the justification for the PS rise to power in the first place was its opposition to the PCP during the high tide of the revolution in 1975. An alliance with the PSD (originally called PPD) was encouraged by some of the PS' sister parties, including the German SPD, but other sister parties did not and neither did the U.S. There were to be many discussions between the PS and PSD during the ensuing three and a half years as well as talks between the PSD and the CDS. The PS did not enter into coalition with the PSD partially because of the intense animosity between Mario Soares and Sá Carneiro (president of the PSD), but mainly because it was anticipated that the popular support for the PSD would diminish from the 24 percent in the 1976 elections if it were not in power. It was thought that the PS and the PSD were sufficiently similar for the PS, being in power, to draw on the political basis of the PSD. Indeed, the PS vetoed the entry of the PSD into the Socialist International to deny it the legitimation of a social democratic party which its name would imply. In any case, in July 1976 the PS formed a government and began to rule in accord with the Constitution which it had a large role in formulating.

In presenting his 260-page Program of the Government, Mario Soares stated, "The government knows what it wants and it is going to achieve a policy that it feels will best serve the national interest. And it is going to do this with courage, with determination, and with vigor."[6] In the 94,000 word document the government of Mario Soares defined nothing less than a model for the modernization of Portugal. The type of society is specified, as are the means to achieve it. In all instances, the theme of the transition to socialism through democracy is stressed. The main elements of the Program are as follows: the construction of a democratic state; the reorganization of the economy through planning; the struggle for economic recovery and financial stabilization; the consolidation of productive structures, combatting unemployment, and the expansion of output; the promotion of greater equity in the distribution of income; meeting the basic needs of the population and promoting the quality of life; and, the affirmation of national independence.[7] The program is in line with the Constitution and further specifies the commitment by the government as well as elaborating the manner in which the changes are to be brought about. The government included a Minister for Planning and Economic Cooperation as well as a Secretary of State for Planning. It produced, during the next two years, extremely detailed plans for each year as well as a medium-range plan for 1977–80.[8] Thus through the Program, and all the commitments it implied, the PS government projected a model of modernization it sought to implement and the instruments for doing so. There was a good deal of optimism that it would succeed in implementing at least part of this, for much of the change had already occurred in the revolution, albeit haphazardly, and this was a government with much legitimacy.

Yet some three years later, by December of 1979, it was clear that little which had been stipulated in the Program had been achieved. The PS model of modernization had not been implemented. Further, through their process of implementation and subsequent reactions to this process, a whole series of changes arising from the revolution, and now enshrined in the Constitution in the items dealing with the transition to socialism, were brought into question. Indeed, in the interim Assembly elections of December 1979, and reinforced in the regular elections of October 1980, a coalition would come to power committed to changing the Constitution. This chapter will provide a description of the political instability which made the implementation of the PS model of modernization impossible, and then will draw conclusions concerning the nature of the political system.

The First Constitutional Government of the minority PS remained in power for 16 months by looking for support to the Left (PCP) on some issues and the Right (PSD and CDS) on others. This was a tremendous balancing act, which hampered its ability to pass and implement legislation as well as threatened its survival as government. For example, if the PS could have the support on some issue of the PCP this meant that it alienated the other two parties; and if it relied on the PSD and/or CDS this meant that it estranged the PCP. It was, in short, a strategy with a limited duration. By late summer 1977 the PCP was in opposition to the government on the agrarian reform issue and was advocating its collapse. What finally brought the First Constitutional Government to an end were the fundamental issues raised in the General State Budget, the Plan for 1978, and the requirement of the International Monetary Fund (IMF) to have broad support from the "political and social forces" in Portugal before negotiating a $50 million standby loan which would open the way for a larger $750 million loan from a number of countries. Thus these three issues comprised most of the major factors in the serious economic situation and pointed out the need for something more than a weak minority government. The parties indicated that if the PS government wanted their support they would expect participation in the government. The PS, calculating that all other coalitions were unlikely and that any government required their participation, refused, and the government was defeated on a vote of confidence of 100 to 159 on December 9, 1977.

The PS minority government would have collapsed sooner had it not been for the active intervention by President Eanes who acted as a mediator between the PS and the other parties. Since the other parties had grown increasingly hostile to the PS which repeatedly stated in an arrogant manner, "either us or chaos," it required the intervention of a higher office to keep the government in power.[9] After the collapse of the First Constitutional Government, the president's role increased as the parties in general, and the PS in particular, showed themselves unable to cooperate and form governments. The president was involved in a month of intense negotiations (the IMF negotiations being in abeyance) to form a second government. The same problem of forming a coalition with either the PCP or the PSD pertained as before, but, incredible as it may seem, a coalition was formed between the PS and the supposedly far-Right CDS which had even voted against the Constitution. The arrangement was not called a coalition but rather a PS government, with the participation of three leading members of the CDS, and several secretaries of state, but in fact it was a coalition. The Program of the Second Constitutional Government was approved in February 1978, with only the PS and CDS voting in favor.

The PS and CDS government was feasible, even if seemingly aberrant, not only because of the involvement of President Eanes but also because the PSD, under the strong and somewhat erratic leadership of Sá Carneiro, was undergoing frequent organizational crises.[10] Thus the PS and CDS government was not kept in power by coherence and ability, but rather by the problems in another key party. It was felt that the PS and CDS in power would draw support from the PSD. However, what happened instead was that Sá Carneiro consolidated his power within the PSD and returned to its presidency in June of 1978. He could then effectively criticize the CDS from the Right for participating in a government which of necessity had to implement unpopular and difficult economic measures. The CDS responded by making a number of demands on the PS, specifically regarding the National Health Service and the Agrarian Reform Law. The CDS also demanded a cabinet reshuffle with particular reference to the Ministry of Agriculture and Fishing. The PS refused, which led to the disappearance of the majority in the Assembly as the CDS would no longer support the government. There being no support the president acted rapidly, and some would say arbitrarily, in dismissing Mario Soares on July 27, 1978.

Following these two negative experiences at party-based government and with no coalitions apparently possible, the president increased his role and formed a government of "independents" with little if any consultation with the parties. He thus called on an individual with slight party identification, Nobre da Costa, to form a government with other independents which would enjoy the confidence of the president. His expectation was that the government would be tolerated if not supported in the Assembly for lack of other options. However, the parties were so little involved in the formation which took place in August that when its Program was presented to the Assembly on September 14, only the PSD and a few independents voted for it. It thus fell, but remained in office until November 21 in the absence of any other government.

President Eanes formed the Fourth Constitutional Government in a similar manner, that is on his own initiative, but with broader consultation which extended to at least the PS, PSD, and CDS. By this time it was clear that there were three hypothetical options: a party coalition, a government initiated by the president, or interim elections. Since the first option was still not possible and the last one generally objectionable for fear on the part of each party at this time that they would lose support, only the second option seemed possible and less undesirable. Thus the government under Carlos Alberto de Mota Pinto took office in December 1978 and its Program was supported in the Assembly by the PS, PSD, and CDS; the PCP voted against it. By April the government showed that it was both quite conservative and neither coherent nor competent. With this government initiated by the president, the PS and PSD had an opportunity to define themselves in opposition to it and discuss possible coalitions. Nothing came of these discussions, but these parties did develop a sense of possible positive results if elections were held. With increasing difficulties in the government and a greater sense of opposition on the part of parties, the government resigned on June 13 rather than face two censure motions. The general split in opposing this Fourth Constitutional Government was Left/Right, but in fact there were tremendous problems with this government and it was generally unpopular. The president attempted once again to initiate another government but this proved impossible and he appointed an interim prime minister (Lourdes Pintassilgo), dissolved the Assembly of the Republic, and prepared for interim elections. These were held on December 2, 1979, and brought to power a right-of-center coalition which was returned to power in the elections of October 1980. The Sixth

Constitutional Government was composed of the Democratic Alliance (AD made of PSD, CDS, and PPM) and had a working majority with 121 deputies versus the PS with 74, the PCP in an alliance with the MDP (APU) with 47, and 7 PSD independents. The AD coalition opposed much of the change brought about through the revolution, guaranteed in the Constitution of 1976, and aspired to in the Program of the First Constitutional Government of the PS.

The three and a half years after July 1976 saw five governments come and go in Portugal. This does not say much for governmental stability and only looks reasonable in the context of the six provisional governments between April 1974 and July 1976. Nor, judging from the analyses of output, does it say much for the productivity of the Assembly of the Republic and the governments.[11] The most serious long-term failings of the three and a half years of constitutional governments are in my view two in number. The first is the low popular opinion of the governments, the regime, and the results of the revolution which will be discussed in the next chapter. The second is that the PS failed to consolidate the gains of the revolution, despite high domestic legitimacy and the international support so that they can be dismantled. Clearly, not all of the changes arising from the revolution could, or maybe even should, have been consolidated, but surely the PS should have formulated a strategy which would have at least ensured the continuation of the more popular and participatory aspects of the revolution. The PS, in my view, confused rhetoric with governing and allowed the opposition to define a broad frontal attack so that all was put into question. By assuming that it was the only party that could govern, by engaging in the "we or chaos" game, the PS made something of a joke of precisely those changes it legitimated itself by supposedly supporting.[12]

The most obvious reason for the governmental instability is of course the fact that the elections of April 25, 1976, gave no party a majority of seats in the Assembly of the Republic. It was thus up to the PS, with the greatest number of seats, to govern on its own or in coalition. There were many possibilities for coalitions which were discussed more or less seriously from early 1977 until the middle of 1979 as the unworkability of the PS government and subsequent unworkability of the nonparty governments was clear. In July of 1977 and then again in March of 1979, a coalition between the PS and PSD was discussed. A coalition between the PS and the PCP was discussed in late 1977 at the time of the collapse of the First Constitutional Government. A coalition between the PSD and the CDS was discussed in May of 1977 and then finally achieved in June of 1979 with the inclusion of the small PPM as well. The larger question is, of course, why it took more than three years of governmental instability and problems of policy implementation before a workable (as opposed to the PS and CDS which were strange bedfellows indeed—even for politics) coalition could be worked out. It would seem that there are two major reasons for the inability to arrange a coalition during this period. One concerns the parties themselves, and the other the larger political institutional framework within which they operate.

There are four main parties that must be considered in discussing politics during the period of the constitutional governments. The only stable, coherent, and consistent (within the terms of its ideology) party was the PCP. At the same time, however, it has shown itself to be intransigent as an orthodox as opposed to Eurocommunist party, thereby lacking the flexibility of the PCI, for example. What is more, the PCP is not trusted by the other parties since its struggle for power during the high tide of the revolution. This party, then, while normally receiving somewhere around 16 percent to 19 percent of the vote, is not really available for partnership in a coalition with the other parties as they are presently constituted in Portugal.

The other three parties were all formed at the time of (shortly before as the PS, or shortly after as the PSD and CDS) the April 25 coup. All of them have been very much the creation and vehicle of one individual or a very limited group of individuals, rather than ongoing organizations which had evolved during struggles and crises. Thus a reading of politics during the three year period is dramatized by a tremendous amount of personality characteristics, personal failings, short term orientations, and reactions of one leader to another. During this three year period there was, after their rapid formation and their marginalization during the revolutionary process, a certain sorting out or shifting of the membership and cadre in each of the parties. The party congress records are not so much about organizations, but rather the personal achievements and failings of the leaders such as Mario Soares, Sá Carneiro, and Freitas do Amaral. This is not, I am sure, the tendency for the newspapers to personalize issues and platforms, but is in fact the case in these young and poorly defined and structured parties. We must remember as well that after 1974 all issues were defined very much to the Left, so that from 1976 the parties have moved toward their real bases which would necessarily be further to the Right by the mere fact that the MFA and the revolution had been replaced by civilian politics and elections. The sorting, then, would involve a great deal of shifting and interaction among very strong personalities. It should also be noted that a new political class came into power after 1976, and as all have noted the lack of preparation of the MFA after 1974, so too can one point to the lack of preparation of these politicians after 1976.[13] Understandably enough, they lacked preparation and experience and gained it after 1976; the cost was instability and subsequent problems. At this point, it might be useful to briefly comment on the three parties.[14]

The PS remains even today the personal creation and instrument of its secretary-general, Mario Soares. During the 1974–75 period it defined itself as a Marxist-oriented party to occupy some of the political ground which would be taken by the PCP. Winning the largest percentage of the vote and thus the largest number of seats in the 1975 and 1976 elections, it defined itself as the "hinge party"; all possible governments would have to include it as the party between the Left and the Right. Its importance and centrality were bolstered by the fact that it enjoyed extremely good and helpful contacts abroad. As a member of the Socialist International since its founding in 1973, the PS served first as party and then government which channeled substantial resources into Portugal. The resources were technical as well as moral and financial, and one would have expected better results from all the help and talent. All documentation and interviews leave one with the impression that Mario Soares and his small coterie could see only short-term strategies which were mainly in response to others. Their party documents are not, in my view, very convincing or workable in Portugal.[15] It was due to the absence of a long-term strategy, a reason for ruling, that such talented young politicians as António Barreto (January 1978) and José Medeiros Ferreira (October 1977) left the government and finally broke with the party itself. The model of modernization was not feasible as the PS lacked the instruments to implement anything so elaborate and forward-looking. Indeed, the PS was barely able to stay in power let alone implement any model of modernization.

The PSD (originally PPD) was very much the creation and vehicle of its President Sá Carneiro until his tragic death in December 1980. It originally attempted to occupy similar ideological space as the PS, but the latter's veto on entering the Socialist International made this difficult. It received little international support and its members were generally critical of the U.S. and Germany for not being more supportive. As the PS discredited the position of the middle Left, the PSD moved further to the Right and showed that there was indeed support which did not, as the PS anticipated, disappear when it was out of power. Until the formation of the Democratic Alliance and Sá Carneiro's death, most of the activities of the PSD must be seen in terms of the personality of its leader. Sá Carneiro struggled with the national leadership, dominated them, went through six congresses, six statutes, two schisms, left the presidency once, threatened it more than once, and in April 1979 saw the departure of 37 of the PSD deputies in the Assembly. With a man such as Sá Carneiro at the head of the party, it is no wonder that understandings and finally a coalition would be difficult to arrange with a personality such as Mario Soares.

Little can be said about the CDS except that it has been a party in search of a constituency and an orientation. It is not a Christian Democratic party nor a classical conservative party, but rather a somewhat technocratic ambiguously-conservative party. It too has been quite "flexible" in that while voting against the Constitution of 1976 the party did enter into a short-term (as it turned out) coalition with the PS. It has, if anything, a weaker organization than the other three parties but the quality of its leadership has been good. The leadership has been largely shared between Freitas do Amaral and Amaro da Costa until the latter's death with Sá Carneiro in 1980. There is not a great deal to differentiate the CDS from the PSD, and thus the role of personalities and short-run strategies would assume greater importance.

This synopsis of the three main parties suggests a changing and accentuated flexibility as might be expected from their newness, a stress on personalities and reactions to personalities, a need for ideological definition, a lack of defined constituencies, and, at least in the case of the PS, a strong reliance on international support. All of this is quite understandable given the lack of party politics in the old regime and the pressures and complexities of the situation since 1974. However, these shortcomings caused serious instability and hampered the effective implementation of policy.

The larger institutional framework was not only a cause and a consequence, in conjunction with the complexity of the post-revolutionary situation and the ambiguity of the parties, of the political instability, but also provided a certain guarantee that this instability would not destroy the regime nor impede all of the socioeconomic changes. That is, governmental instability was in a certain sense encouraged by the institutional framework but the negative consequences are somewhat limited by it. Arising from the Party Pact of February 1976 and further defined and elaborated in the Constitution is the provision that the parliamentary system of a government with its basis of support in the Assembly of the Republic is not the whole system. Rather, the political system is at least semi-presidential and, for the period while the Revolutionary Council survived, "supervised."[16] This system and its inherent implications provided a handy excuse for the politicians who seemed unable to come to agreements between 1976 and late 1979. They realized that their actions would not destroy the system, although they were quick to blame other parties for the same behavior.

The political system defined in the Constitution of 1976 is semipresidential (or bipolar). The president who was popularly elected was also chief of staff of the armed forces and president of the Revolutionary Council. The president lacked executive powers except with regard to the armed forces. However, in conjunction with the Revolutionary Council, with which he was to consult, his formal powers were extensive. They included: the nomination of the prime minister after "consulting with the Revolutionary Council and the parties represented in the Assembly, 'holding in mind the electoral results' " (article 190); dismissal of the prime minister; dissolution of the assembly (article 136); an explicit veto which can be overridden by a majority or in some cases two thirds (artice 139); declaration of war, a state of siege, or emergency. In addition, due to the ambiguity of the text, the president also had a pocket veto and could dismiss the prime minister even though he might hold the confidence of the Assembly. The president presided at the Revolutionary Council which had exclusive jurisdiction regarding the armed forces, was the constitutional tribunal, and served as a council for the president. As seen with the Third, Fourth, and Fifth Constitutional Governments, the president could in effect break and make governments. They might not survive the Assembly, but he could take the initiative in forming them. These extensive powers of the president might well have remained latent and residual if the parties had been better able to cooperate in the period of 1977–79. However, in that situation of instability the president was forced to draw on his Constitutional powers.[17] Thus despite governmental instability, the political system continued functioning through the intervention and supervision of the president.

The president, in the person of General Ramalho Eanes, represented the continuation of the MFA in that he was linked to them and in the fall of 1975, was instrumental in ensuring the survival of the system envisioned to some extent in the Program of the MFA and promoted by Major Melo Antunes. What is more, he was elected in a four-way race for the presidency by some 62 percent of the population. His legitimacy, then, from the revolution and the population was more comprehensive than any other individual or party in the country.

The MFA also continued in the constitutional system through the Revolutionary Council. This too was included in the Party Pact, which provided for the continued inclusion of the Revolutionary Council until at least the first constitutional revision which could only become possible in 1981, after the end of the first full legislature. It was designed to supervise the political system and to provide for the continuing progressive orientation of the regime despite the political parties. Formally, it assists the president, supervises the government, and judges on the constitutionality of legislation. It is not popularly elected, but rather represents a continuation of the MFA and recognizes the important role they played in forming a new regime and socioeconomic system. In fact, the Revolutionary Council acts as a flywheel to offset the increased pressures from the Right. It has played this role less because of legal provisions and more because of the personal relationships between members on it and the President.[18] Thus the combination of the president, so far in the person of General Ramalho Eanes, and the CR has meant that the politicians could be allowed a certain amount of flexibility or learning experiences in working with the new political system. The PS would appear to have handled this not particularly well and has found itself out of power. What is more, by being identified with so much of the revolutionary change, as written into the Constitution, the PS has also put these changes into question. Even so, the democratic regime has continued even if one of the main institutions guaranteeing it is not elected at all.

President Eanes has remained aloof from the political parties and has rejected all proposals for the revision of the system into a more presidential pattern.[19] By defining himself as guarantor of the Constitution, in lieu of the PS being able to act in this capacity, he has become identified with the Left since the Constitution guarantees the results of the revolution. Much of the stuff of politics since the interim parliamentary elections of December 2, 1979, which brought the AD to power and the normal parliamentary elections of October 5, 1980, which reaffirmed their mandate has been the battle between the president and the government. This is the case because the candidate of the AD for the presidential elections of December 7, 1980, General Soares Carneiro, with some 40 percent of the votes trailed President Eanes with 56 percent. Therefore, the governments (Sixth to Eighth Constitutional Governments) were dominated by the AD and the presidency by Ramalho Eanes. Chapter Seven will analyze the conflicts by looking to the important topic of constitutional revision.

The revolutionary changes brought about between 1974 and 1976 were not consolidated by the PS, which claimed legitimacy both from the revolution and from its opposition to the PCP in the struggle for power. It was unable to take advantage of its legitimacy and the international support (party to party and state to state) to consolidate the model of modernization defined in the Constitution of 1976 and further elaborated on in the PS Government Program of July 1976. Rather, the government drifted, equivocated, and fell within two years. As the parties were subsequently unable to form coalitions, the president used his formal powers to form governments and finally call interim elections a year early. Due to the inability of the PS to consolidate the gains of the revolution, the president and the CR became identified as the organs of sovereignty responsible for the Constitution and the changes there guaranteed. Politics had thus come to center on the question of the nature of a modernizing strategy and the composition and relationship of the organs of sovereignty (or structures of the state). In the next chapter the nature of popular support for the new regime will be analyzed, and in Chapter Seven the processes presaging change in the economy and society will be examined.

Notes

1. See the appendix for OECD comparative figures.
2. The World Bank, *Portugal: Current and Prospective Economic Trends* (Washington, D.C.: The World Bank, November 1978), p. i.
3. Ibid., p. ii.
4. On the economy and the IMF see, respectively, Paul Krugman and Jorge Braga de Macedo, "The Economic Consequences of the April 25th Revolution," pp. 53–87, and Barbara Stallings, "Portugal and the IMF: The Political Economy of Stabilization," in *Portugal Since the Revolution: Economic and Political Perspectives*, eds. Jorge Braga de Macedo and Simon Serfaty (Boulder, Colorado: Westview Press, 1981), pp. 101–35.
5. Dr. Jorge Miranda, *Expresso*, 1 April 1977.
6. *O Jornal*, 6 August 1976.
7. Programa do Governo, *Apresentação para apreciação, debate, encerramento do debate* (Lisbon: Imprensa Nacional, 1976). For a summary see *Portugal Information* (August-September 1976): 2–14.
8. See Ministério de Plano e Coordenção Economica, *Plano Para 1977* (Lisbon: Imprensa Nacional, 1977). And the 9 volumes of *Plano de Médio Prazo* done by the Ministério do Plano e Coordenação Economica, Secretária de Estado do Planeamento (Lisbon: Imprensa Nacional, 1977).
9. Avelino Rodrigues, et al., *Abril nos Quartéis de Novembêro* (Lisbon: Livraria Bertrand, 1979). pp. 196–97.
10. There is a good review of Sá Carneiro's stewardship of the party, and the many crises, in *Expresso*, 3 January 1981, p. 2. After his tragic death in late 1980 there was an outpouring of books on Sá Carneiro. For a good review of five of these books see José Antonio Saraiva, "Cinco vezes Sá Carneiro," revista of *Expresso*, 22 May 1982.
11. For descriptions of the "productivity" see *Expresso*, 1 September 1979, p. R,1 and *O Jornal*, 13 September 1979, p. 6.
12. The discussion of Juan J. Linz on legitimacy, efficacy, and effectiveness is relevant to this section but as the system has not yet "broken down" I will not go into it here. See Juan J. Linz, *The Breakdown of Democratic Regimes: Crisis, Breakdown, and Reequilibration* (Baltimore: The Johns Hopkins University Press, 1978), pp. 16–22.

13. For some very insightful comments on this political class by one of its members see, for example, A. L. Sousa Franco, "Reflexão sobre a class política," *O Jornal*, 10 November 1978, p. 6.

14. For other discussions on the parties see, for example, Ben Pimlott, "Parties and Voters in the Portuguese Revolution: The Elections of 1975 and 1976," *Parliamentary Affairs* 30 (Winter, 1977): 35–58; Howard J. Wiarda, "Spain and Portugal," in *Western European Party Systems* ed., Peter Merkl (N.Y.: The Free Press, 1980); Kenneth Maxwell, "Strategies and Tactics of the Portuguese Communist Party," in *Eurocommunism*, ed. George Schwab (Westport: Greenwood Press, 1968), pp. 269–302; Tom Gallagher, "Portugal's Bid for Democracy: The Role of the Socialist Party," *West European Politics* 2 (May 1979): 198–217; José Durão Barroso, "Quelques éléments pour l'étude des partis politiques portugais: organisation; clivage idéologique; bibliographie sélective," mimeographed (November 1982); and Joaquim Aguiar, *A Ilusão do Poder: Análise do sistema partidário português, 1976–1982* (Lisbon: Publicações Dom Quixote, 1982).

15. See for example Partido Socialista's "base document" *Dez Anos para Mudar Portugal: Proposta PS para os Anos 80* (Lisbon: Portugal Socialista, December 1978), pp. 1–91.

16. There is a particularly useful discussion on this theme in Marcelo Rebelo de Sousa, *Direito Constitucional* (Braga: Livraria Cruz, 1979), pp. 346–56. For a rather critical view of these same points see Marcello Caetano, *Constituições Portuguesas* (Lisbon: Verbo, 1978), pp. 125–57.

17. For a good analysis of this process see *Expresso*, 17 January 1981, pp. R 3–5.

18. This information is based on interviews with members and staff of the Revolutionary Council in 1977, 1978, 1979, and 1981.

19. This information is based on interviews with proponents of such plans, politicians, and journalists in 1978, 1979, and 1981.

6

Attitudes on the Revolution, Regime, and Governments

This chapter is primarily a report on the results of a national survey conducted in continental Portugal (i.e., excluding the Azores and Madeira)in the early spring of 1978.[1] Polls have their utility depending not only on their technical sophistication and the sample covered, but also according to the political context in which they are conducted. In stable democratic regimes they are certainly useful in determining the attitudes of sectors of the population, most frequently with regard to voting, but as these regimes are stable even substantial shifts in opinion do not raise questions as to the continuity of the regime. In authoritarian regimes, on the other hand, polls can again provide data on opinions, but as these regimes do not link popular attitudes to government, by means of elections, they are at the most suggestive.[2]

I believe that the results of the poll reported in this chapter are fundamental to an understanding of the future of the regime in Portugal, and consequently, the pattern of modernization to be pursued. The last chapter stated that the general outline of the post–1976 regime is still in flux, due to its relative immaturity and the very different positions taken by the political parties and other political institutions. As the attitudes of the population are today linked to government through elections they do indeed matter. But beyond the elections the attitudes of the population, as indicated in this poll, are important for at least two other reasons: First, groups and movements might find support in the population to dismantle or, much less likely, accelerate the changes initiated in 1974. Second, any regime in Portugal today is likely to take measures to rationalize some aspects of the socioeconomic system, and such measures would be supported or opposed depending on the attitudes of the population. In sum, the attitudes of the population matter today in Portugal for they are linked in a variety of ways to the regime, and this regime is in the process of definition.

The survey was conducted in the early spring of 1978. This was slightly less than two years after the liberal democratic regime as defined in the Constitution had been implemented, three months into the Second Constitutional Government (PS and CDS), and at a time when the population was being inundated with information on the IMF negotiations, the economic crisis, and the possible entry into the EEC. It was obvious that there were problems of political instability as the PS government had fallen on a vote of confidence and President Eanes was beginning to assert his residual powers which would lead to three governments formed on his initiative. It was not a period of reactionary activity, but one in which the nature of the regime and the socioeconomic system remained in question. It was a time of flux and, therefore, a period that was particularly rich in general information and an opportune time to conduct a survey.

The overall question informing the material to be discussed in this chapter is whether the Portuguese would support, or even allow, the dismantling of the regime and the structural changes initiated in 1974. In the last chapter we say that politically this is possible. The attitudes surveyed in this chapter must be understood in the context of recent events in Portugal. Portugal lived under a conservative authoritarian regime for almost a half century, the standard of living and educational levels are the lowest of Western Europe, massive emigration has displaced a large percentage of the younger and more active sectors of the working population, and the Portuguese have a reputation for political passivity and apathy which may not have been created by the Estado Novo. The revolution promised much and only partially delivered. These data, for those who have closely studied Portugal and the Portuguese, are not startling. As usual with surveys, the data go to reaffirm much of what is already known by informed observers. In what follows the tables will be presented for the whole sample unstratified by sex, class, age, region, and political affiliation. These are of course available in the printout and when some particularly interesting variations occur by any of these stratifying factors, or if something might have been anticipated but did not appear, there will be further elaboration.

In response to a question on what people are proudest of in Portugal, with first, second, and third priorities, we find the following distribution.

Table 6.1   Which of these aspects are we Portuguese proudest of?

Feel pride for which aspects	1st	2nd	3rd	Total
(percentage)				
Contribution to civilization	10	6	2	18
Government	1	1	2	4
Discoveries	14	8	4	26
Revolution of April 25	15	6	2	23
Literature	1	2	4	7
Qualities of our people	5	8	8	21
Religious life	3	2	2	7
Constitution of 1976	1	6	3	10
Artistic wealth	–	1	5	6
Decolonization	1	2	3	6
Armed forces	1	3	5	9
Nothing	12	2	2	16
No response	37	53	58	–

What emerges most clearly is the pride in historical and cultural factors and the low emphasis on results of the revolution such as government (4 percent), decolonization (6 percent), and the Constitution of 1976 (10 percent). We might note the strong similarity in results if we compare these to a survey done in 1973 using a similar question.[3] At that time a total of 4 percent mentioned the political system and another 18 percent mentioned government and authority. If anything, then, the government is held in less regard today than in the past, and the main criteria for pride in Portugal concern history, the people, and culture in general. We must note, however, that a total of 23 percent, with 15 percent citing it first, gave the revolution of April 25 as something to be proud of. In general, then, the Portuguese do recognize that the revolution was worthy of pride.

However, when we begin to ask the questions about the results of the revolution we find indications of something less than pride. An overwhelming majority are aware that changes did take place in Portugal after April 25 as indicated in Table 6.2:

Table 6.2 Did anything change in the country with the revolution of April 25, 1974?

Was there change?	Total	By Social Classes			
		Upper	Upper Middle	Lower Middle	Lower
Yes	72	87	86	77	53
No	11	5	8	7	19
No response	17	8	6	16	28

Only 53 percent of the lower class felt that something had changed with the revolution. Of the overall 11 percent reporting that nothing had changed, the elaborations they gave are the following: "everything remained the same": 30 percent; "the situation didn't improve": 26 percent; 44 percent didn't give any reason at all. We then asked a question as to whether the changes at the national level were for the better, worse, or insignificant. The results given in Table 6.3 indicate that while politics and liberty are very highly evaluated, in general the aspects concerning society and economic factors were the same or worse.

Table 6.3 Has change been for the better or worse in the following areas?

Aspects of national life	for better +	no change	worse −	don't know
(percentage)				
Morals	10	15	47	28
Politics	33	7	26	34
The economy	3	6	61	30
Salaries	44	8	25	23
Religion	5	48	20	27
Education/teaching	11	17	40	32
Housing	8	15	52	25
Liberty	51	4	21	24
Development/progress	16	23	28	34
Production	5	9	48	38
No response	30	36	24	−
Average	19	15	37	29

As the bottom line shows, the average was overwhelmingly in the direction of changes being for the worse. And, lest the positive evaluation regarding salaries deceive us, we must look to the results from a question on the impact of the revolution on the individual's own situation.

Table 6.4 indicates that half the population interviewed did not consider that their personal situation had changed; only 6 percent did not respond to this question. What is more we can see that those reporting the least amount of change for the better and the most change for the worst were in the lower classes.

Table 6.4   Has anything changed in your life with April 25?

| Classes | By Socioeconomic Class | | | |
	Change for Better	Change for Worse	No Change	No Response
Upper	24	26	42	8
Upper middle	19	26	53	2
Lower middle	20	22	51	7
Lower	13	30	50	7
Average	19	26	49	6

This question was followed by an open-ended one in which the respondent could indicate the specific aspects of his personal life that had either improved or deteriorated. These data are found in Table 6.5.

Table 6.5   What has changed in personal life and is it for the better or worse?

Changes	For the better	For the worse
(percentage)		
Salaries	53	3
Liberty of expression	23	1
Return from colonies	–	9
Cost of living	–	51
Unemployment	–	18
Everything better	7	–
Everything worse	–	16

Again, the results are mixed. Except for freedom of expression, the overall tendency is toward the negative side for the cost of living counters the improvement in salaries. Generally, then, our respondents indicated that the results of the revolution were not impressive.

The overall sense conveyed by our respondents regarding the changes in politics and society arising from the revolution might best be illustrated by Table 6.6. In response to a question on whether or not there is a crisis in Portuguese society we find that the vast majority felt there was such a crisis.

Table 6.6   Do you think there is a crisis in Portuguese society?

Yes	63
No	5
Don't know	28
No response	4

There was also another open-ended question on the most serious aspects of the crisis. The overwhelming responses concerned economic matters such as the lack of jobs and the increase in the cost of living. This clearly reflects the Portuguese people's concern with the economic situation which they feel originated in the revolution of April 25, 1974.

Even though the main preoccupation would appear to be with personal economies, we can notice a conservative makeup as suggested in Table 6.7. In response to a question on the objective of the government in the next few years that they considered most important, we find the overwhelming emphasis is on peace (45 percent) and order and stability (11 percent).

Table 6.7   What is the most important objective for the government in the next few years?

Equality	14
Order and stability	11
Socialism	10
Peace	45
Liberty	4
Development	10
Don't know	5
No response	1

The main themes of the revolution were equality, development, and socialism, but the 13 years of wars in Africa and the subsequent political instability suggested that order and stability as well as peace were closer to the population's priorities. It might be noted that whereas peace was indicated as the highest priority for 19 percent of the respondents in the upper class, this gradually ascended to 68 percent for those in the lower classes. It is also worth noting the very few "don't know" and "no responses" to this question. It seems to me indicative of the overall attitude paradigm characteristic of the Portuguese people. That is, there is a crisis, it is characterized mainly in economic terms, the people are afraid of instability and the possibility of violence. It seems that the people are giving the highest priority to a peaceful evolution, even though it need not imply development, much less socialism.

This same point may be illustrated very forcefully if we look at the data displayed in Table 6.8 concerning which government or regime governed the country best. We can see the remarkable value given to the old regime (a total of 35 percent) in comparison with all the regimes between 1974 and 1978 (21 percent). What is particularly dramatic is a low 9 percent for Mario Soares after more than a year and a half in office. It is barely above the 8 percent for Vasco Conçalves, who was considered the cause of the haphazard process of decolonization and the economic problems arising from the nationalizations. Thus in comparison with the present the old regime doesn't look too bad at all.

Table 6.8 Which of the following governments or regimes governed the country best?

	(percentage)
Salazar	7
Caetano	28
P. Carlos (1 Provisional)	1
V. Gonçavles (2–5 Provisional)	8
Pinheiro de Azevedo (6 Provisional)	3
Mario Soares (1–2 Constitutional)	9
Don't know	31
No response	13

In response to an open question on why the respondents thought a government or regime was best, the data indicated that while the government of Mario Soares was given credit for guaranteeing the Constitution, promoting liberty and the like, all of these were of an order of 10 percent, whereas the economic preference of the earlier regime was around 50 percent. These data do not say much for the regard in which the new regime is held, a point which is even more dramatic if we include data from a survey done late in 1978 at the time of the formation of the Fourth Constitutional Government.[4]

Table 6.9 What confidence do you have in the following governments to resolve the problems of the country?

Constitutional governments	Much	Some	Little	None	Don't know/ no response
(percentage)					
I Government	9	22	12	24	33
II Government	3	20	16	28	33
III Government	6	20	11	25	38
IV Government	6	21	6	20	47
Average	6	21	11	24	38

We can see that while only 31% had some or much confidence in the First Constitutional Government it still ranked higher than the other three, indicating a decreasing confidence. On the basis of these data the population obviously had some reservations regarding the governments of the new regime.

The regime type, as well as the socioeconomic format of the system, is defined in the Constitution of 1976. In order to gauge the degree of awareness of the institutional format, we asked a number of questions concerning the Constitution. The responses reflect the very low awareness of the population about the Constitution. When offered three different statements and asked to indicate whether these were in agreement or not with the Constitution, 52 percent reported that they didn't know and another 5 percent did not respond. Twelve percent picked the wrong response, leaving therefore the total of 32 percent that chose the statement in agreement with the Constitution. In short, despite the tremendous amount of publicity and discussion concerning the formulation and implementation of the Constitution, less than one-third of our respondents could choose the only statement in agreement with it.

Not only were our respondents unfamiliar with the Constitution, but, as a new and generally unknown document it was not considered inviolable. We asked a question as to under what circumstances the Constitution could be suspended and the results are indicated in Table 6.10 below.

Table 6.10   In which of the following circumstances can the Constitution be suspended?

Conditions/Class	According to class				
	Total	Upper	Upper Middle	Lower Middle	Lower
(percentage)					
War	9	16	12	8	6
Lack of food	8	13	10	7	6
High inflation	5	5	13	3	1
High external debt	4	8	9	2	1
Parties not cooperating	11	18	15	12	5
Never	13	33	24	12	3
Don't know	56	23	32	60	76
No response	4	5	3	4	6

(More than one response possible so percent more than 100)

Again with the many "don't know" responses we can see that the people did not have much of an opinion as to the Constitution. What is most important, however, is that only 13 percent reported that the Constitution could never be suspended. This is very close to the 11 percent who reported that it could be suspended when the parties were not getting along and, as reported in the last chapter, this was the case for most of the time under the Constitutional Governments I–V. We might also note that the lower one goes down the class scale the lower the percentage of those who reported that the Constitution could never be suspended.

In order to understand what the respondents expected from a government, we asked a number of questions concerning the qualities of the governors as well as the institutions necessary to have a democracy. Table 6.11 displays responses to an open-ended question in which we asked for the three principal qualities of a person to govern the country.

Table 6.11   What do you think are the three principal qualities for one who is to govern the country at this time?

	(percentage)
Honesty	23
Courage/firmness	14
Competence	12
Dedication to people	11
Intelligence	7
A-partyness	6
Energy	5
Sincerity/coherence	5
Democratic attitude	5
No response	51

What is obvious, of course, is the very low percentage (5 percent) reporting a democratic attitude. Qualities such as honesty, firmness/courage, intelligence—indeed most of the other qualities do not imply a democratic attitude.

In order to gauge what the respondents felt to be the institutions required for a democracy, we asked a question on precisely this topic, and the results were reported in Table 6.12.

Table 6.12   Which institution is necessary if Portugal is to be a democratic country?

	(percentage)
President of the Republic	24
Neighborhood groups	2
Political parties	18
Organized armed forces	5
A single party	5
Other	2
Don't know	40
No response	4

With the exception of political parties (18 percent) none of the other institutions imply a democratic political format. Interestingly enough, the "no response" was extremely low but we found that the "don't know" was four times as high for the lower class as for the upper and upper-middle class (15 percent versus 63 percent). It seems quite clear from both Tables 6.11

and 6.12 that the Portuguese at this date lacked a set definition on either the personal or institutional requirements of a
democratic order.

Some further appreciation of this point may be conveyed
by the results reported in Tables 6.13 and 6.14. In Table 6.13
we see that most of our respondents felt that political parties
were indeed necessary for a democracy. However, Table 6.14
reflects that only one half of our respondents felt that political
parties bring benefits for the population.

Table 6.13   How necessary are political parties for democracy?

	(percentage)
Very necessary	33
Slightly necessary	25
Not necessary	15
Don't know/no response	27

Table 6.14   Do you think political parties bring benefits for the people?[5]

	(percentage)
Bring many benefits	10
Bring some benefits	38
Do not bring benefits	25
Actually counteract benefits	13
Don't know/no response	14

These data are understandable if we remember the institutions' brief period of implementation and the political instability described in the last chapter. The data displayed below in
Tables 6.15 and 6.16 are also easily comprehensible if we recall
the long period under which the Portuguese lived in a conservative authoritarian regime. These data belie the image that
some might have had of the Portuguese revolution, but are
consistent with our description of the process as one in which
the institutions of the old regime disintegrated. Quite simply
the data show that the population is not heavily involved in political activities and considers itself to be ineffective in these
same matters.

Table 6.15   In which of these political activities are you involved or participate?

Political Activities	
Cadre of party	3
Member of party	5
Assist in distributing propaganda	4
Attend rallies	14
Read, hear, or see information	87
No response	5

Table 6.16   In your opinion, do you think you can be involved in the resolution of national or regional problems that concern you?

	Total	Upper	Upper Middle	Lower Middle	Lower
Yes	16	32	26	15	7
No	71	61	67	68	79
No response	13	7	6	18	15

What we can see from these data is the low number (16 percent) of our respondents who thought they could be effectively involved. What is more, this sense of efficacy drops by 50 percent between the upper and lower-middle class and is halved again between the lower-middle and the lower class.

The data reported in this chapter are unambiguous and are supported in other surveys.[6] They are easily understandable, given the history of the country under the old regime, the oft-referred to political apathy of the Portuguese population, the chaotic and unstructured revolutionary process between 1974 and 1976, and the political instability between 1976 and 1980. What these data indicate is that the population by and large does not yet adhere very closely to the new institutions nor think very highly of the revolution. Thus, while voting turnout is high (87 percent turnout in the December 1979 interim Assembly elections, and 84 percent in the October and December 1980 elections for the Assembly and presidency, but down to 79 percent in the April 1983 interim Assembly elections) it tends to be formalistic and does not imply other involvements, such as work in the parties. The population is disenchanted with the promises of the revolution, and while they support the president do not necessarily expect him to act in a democratic manner. It is clear that while some groups (mainly the PCP and others further to the Left) would struggle to prevent changes in the Constitution and to retain the gains made by the revolution, the vast majority of the population would not. A number of our questions indicated that the respondents had a certain amount of pride in Portugal and wanted to see something novel and unique created, but they did not feel that the institutions and processes presently functioning were those that they were hoping for. In short, a government such as the AD would find little general constraint in the population for a significant regression. A president, receiving support from the same population, may be committed to preventing these changes, but this is not because of some specific mandate on the part of the population which has a consciousness of this process. From these data it would appear that the Portuguese have changed less than one might anticipate during the revolutionary period; their attitudes—both socially and politically—are very similar to the results found in the survey conducted in 1973.

Notes

1. The survey was supported by a Rockefeller Foundation Fellowship in Conflict in International Relations and administered for me by NORMA (Sociedade de Estudos para o Desenvolvimento de Empresas). The questionnaire contained forty-six main items, sixteen sub items, and eleven open-ended questions as well as a series of items to define the sex, age, class, and region of the respondent. Dr. Mário Bacalhau and I elaborated the questionnaire utilizing samples from others, including most specifically those of Juan J. Linz in his work on Spain. Professor Jerome Black of McGill University was most helpful in the formulation of the items. Following two pretests, the questionnaire was administered to 2,000 individuals in a national representative sample of Metropolitan Portugal. The universe is the whole of the population over eighteen years of age who were selected according to a random sampling strategy elaborated by NORMA which gives all individuals in the universe the same probability of selection. The sample was stratified according to region (seven) and the size of village or town (eleven categories). The work began in the field on March 8, 1978, and was completed on April 24. The survey is discussed in detail in Thomas Bruneau and Mário Bacalhau, *Os Portugueses e a Política Quatro Anos Depois do 25 de Abril* (Lisbon: Editorial Meseta, 1978). Appendix I is the questionnaire and Appendix II describes the methodology of the survey and data analysis.

2. I have also conducted a survey in an authoritarian regime, Brazil, and thus do not intend to denigrate their utility for certain types of questions. See Thomas C. Bruneau, *The Church in Brazil: The Politics of Religion* (Austin: University of Texas Press, 1982), pp. 161–72.

3. IPOPE, *Os Portugueses e a Política–1973* (Lisbon: Moraes Editores, 1973). Dr. Bacalhau worked on this survey as well and we intentionally used a number of the same questions for purposes of comparison.

4. Mário Bacalhau, *Eanes: A Solução?* (Lisbon: Heptagono, 1979), p. 61.

5. Ibid., p. 69.

6. My colleague Bacalhau continues to conduct surveys. See also the results of surveys periodically published in *Expresso*. For example, March 1 and 15, 1980.

7

Modernization and Regime-Formation: Internal and External Constraints

The traditional approach to modernization in Portugal, which in many ways was a strategy to discourage modernization, became untenable by the late 1960s and was modified in some sectors. Foreign investment was encouraged, industrialization expanded, and trade patterns shifted. However, the nexus of the traditional policy, the maintenance of the colonial empire, was reasserted and the vocation of Portugal as a colonial empire reaffirmed. There was a certain amount of unintegrated planning but this was not fully implemented, due to the shortage of resources caused by the costs of the colonial wars.[1] The commitment to remain in Africa frustrated economic and social development; it was also the main reason for the failure of Marcello Caetano's efforts at liberalization. In earlier chapters it has been argued that the coup of April 25, 1974, resulted from the regime's intransigence in a situation widely recognized to be in crisis. The approach to modernization was perceived as a failure, and the enthusiasm with which April 25 was greeted by the vast majority of the population is a good indication of the depth and scope of this perception. However, it has been pointed out as well that there was no single group with sufficient power to implement its model of modernization. Rather, the stalemate of forces, in which foreign actors were heavily involved, gave rise to a political system in which the interests of the population are recognized through elections and interest group activities. That is, the democratic compromise has in fact institutionalized uncertainty. Conflicts are now worked out through political structures in which different groups and classes have varying strengths and resources. While the revolutionary activity of 1974–76 brought about substantial change in most areas of economy, polity, and society, these changes were by no means integrated into a coherent strategy of modernization and they are not definitive. Except for decolonization, virtually all of these changes can be rolled back. Further, the exact nature of the regime itself is not definitive as a particular conjuncture of actors and events led to its formation in 1976, and the dynamic of politics since then has created conflicting tendencies for change. This chapter will link some internal and external influences on modernization and regime-formation in Portugal in the period of 1976–82 and attempt to show the extent of flux and the likely direction of change.

The overall orientation of the Constitution of 1976, as reemphasized in the PS Government Programme of August 1976, is to move the society increasingly toward a socialist system. The private sector is to disintegrate through such processes as nationalizations, abolition of latifundia, and the formation and growth of workers' organizations. However, despite this overall commitment and the detailed stipulation of much of the processes and structures in its 312 items, the Constitution left the precise implementation of the system to ordinary law. It was thus the responsibility of governments by means of legislation to provide the precise details and operation of this socialist system. The discussion in previous chapters has made it obvious that the goals of this Constitution in a country as underdeveloped as Portugal, with a functioning liberal democratic system of elections, were unlikely to be implemented. The goals or aspirations were derived from a revolutionary period in which both the PS and the PCP were predominant. The implementation would require the coherence of at least one of these parties while in power. This has not been the case, however; the PCP has never achieved power, and the PS has not shown coherence. The checkered actions of the PS between mid-1976 and mid-1978 are suggestive of the erratic behavior, and the coalition with the presumably rightist CDS is ample proof of the lack of coherence. Between late 1979 and late 1982, the AD was in power, and the three parties which constitute it were not in sympathy with the general tenor of the Constitution of 1976. Indeed, both the president of the PSD—Francisco Sá Carneiro—and the president of the CDS—Freitas do Amaral—wrote books and other documents with replacement constitutions. Of course, in the case of the latter, we might recall that the CDS did not vote in favor of the Constitution in the Constituent Assembly in 1976.

When the AD came to power in the interim elections of 1979 and were confirmed in the regular elections in 1980, it anticipated constitutional revision either through the Assembly or the presidency. If the sufficient two-thirds vote required for revision could not be obtained in the Assembly, the AD expected that their candidate for president—General Soares Carneiro—could ensure revision through a referendum. However, the AD failed to achieve the two-thirds required, nor was Soares Carneiro elected. Therefore, with the reelection of President Ramalho Eanes in December 1980, there was a constant tension between the government, headed in the Seventh and Eighth Constitutional Governments by Prime Minister Francisco Balsemão, and the president.

Revision touched upon many aspects of the Constitution, and the proposed changes would leave but 34 of the 312 items intact.[2] The document prepared by the subcommittee on revision and presented in May 1982 to the deputies has indeed a different tenor from the Constitution of 1976. Socialism, collectivism, and the emphasis on workers and structural reform have been downplayed. Liberalism, the individual, and growth are emphasized. However, in my view (and the view of those involved), these items are not crucial. The "transition to socialism" remains, but this item and others of a programmatic character have been dead letters since 1976 and are likely to continue to remain that way. Very simply, as the insightful and extremely well-connected Marcelo Rebelo de Sousa has shown, practice in socioeconomic matters has not been in accord with the Constitution.[3] In my view this was due to the ambiguity of the Constitution itself, the changing political balance of forces, and the reality of the international context and Portugal's place in it. The ambiguity is well-covered by Rebelo de Sousa; here I should like to deal with a few added points on the changing balance of forces and the international context.

In the revolutionary period the political parties were not the most important political actors. This place was reserved for the MFA and its relationship with the PCP. A broad variety of groups emerged in the confusion of the time and gave a certain orientation or cachet to the Portuguese revolution. Today, however, these groups have by and large disappeared, and the few remaining have little influence. The labor movement remains one of the most active; it is also still under the control, or at least orientation, of the PCP. But in lieu of the spontaneous and innovative outburst of the revolutionary period, the movement functions to maintain the gains of the workers through nonrevolutionary activities of strikes as in other Western European countries. The labor movement has not been very effective: the earning power of the Portuguese workers has in fact dropped since 1975, which gives some idea of the movement's relative strength.[4] It should be mentioned that although the PCP predominates in the labor movement through the CGTP-IN, it is contested by the UGT which incorporates unions associated with the PS and PSD. The labor movement lives on in Portugal and functions fairly well within the framework of a liberal democratic regime; however, it is split and while at times disruptive is not very strong in exerting its political power.[5]

The situation with the owners' organizations is the opposite. During the revolution businessmen and industrialists were on the defensive, both for their identification with the old regime and because capitalists are not popular when socialism is on the rise. By 1976 groups representing owners in industry, commerce, and agriculture were reorganizing and increasingly affirmatory. By November 1977, at the time of the negotiations with the IMF, not only were the opposition political parties demanding a role in government in exchange for their support of the IMF package, but the sectoral organization of the industrialists (CIP—Confederation of Portuguese Industry) was seeking a change in the Constitution in line with the role that they felt had to be played by private domestic capital. Specifically, they demanded restrictions on the rights of workers, a clearer definition of obligations and privileges of workers and managers, and the rapid indemnization of those who have been expropriated. Since that time the sectoral organizations of farm owners (CAP—Confederation of Portuguese Agriculture) and businessmen (CCC—Confederation of Chambers of Commerce), as well as the CIP, have been active in holding conferences, publishing statements and books, and lobbying in government and the bureaucracy. In an about-face the labor organizations are comparatively circumscribed today, whereas the owners' organizations are active and have been well-received by recent governments, although there remain differences of orientation among these organizations.

Because of the importance of the owners in the present political context, it is useful to see what their priorities are in defining a pattern of modernization. In January of 1979 the CIP, CAP, and CCC held a conference and founded a Council of Economic Activities.[6] This was an important and large conference, which considered almost a score of prepared papers on various sectors of industry, agriculture, and business. The papers themselves are a useful summary of the sad state of the Portuguese economy and are, as one would anticipate, from the perspective of private domestic capital. They argue, for example, that the economy will not become dynamic unless "we change the collectivist institutional economic system incoherently laid down by the confusing constitution, drawn up and approved in a conditioned climate of anti-democratic pressure."[7] They demand the reorientation of the economy toward a market economy in which private enterprise is neither suffocated nor subservient to the state. Among their specific suggestions are the following: eliminate from the Constitution all provisions expressing a collectivist and bureaucratic intention; adjust the principles of social and economic organization to market laws and the norms of equilibrium between capital and labor prevalent in other parts of Europe; radically alter Law 46/77 which prohibits Portuguese enterprise from involvement in sectors such as banking and insurance; review the juridical situation concerning indemnification of owners of nationalized and expropriated property; and modify the labor legislation substantially particularly regarding strikes, lockouts, contracts, collective bargaining, and the powers of workers' committees. There are a total of 13 main suggestions and, if implemented, they would redefine the economic system into a market economy with limited state involvement.

In addition to the importance of these sector organizations and their adherents involved in the economy and in politics today, it is worth noting that their argument for a redefinition of the socioeconomic system is couched very strongly in terms of external factors. They view entry into the European Economic Community as a "national project" to be done quickly and thoroughly. They stress in particular that the EEC is a "free enterprise economy based on the market and not restricting investors." As an economist close to these groups put it: "The nature ascribed to economic organization in the Portuguese Constitution is not adjustable to the market-oriented type of economy with a strong private sector, which is the system in the EEC countries. . . . Bearing in mind the implications of accession to the EEC, there is undoubtedly a strong case for a revision of the Constitution aimed at eliminating the present discrepancies as regards economic organization."[8] Thus an internal strategy is related to external factors which are used for justification and legitimation. The strongest indicator of the importance of external factors is the simple statistic cited twice in the Conclusions of the conference to the effect that Portugal represents but 3 percent of an enlarged EEC population and 1 percent of its GNP. Portugal, having lost its colonies, passed through a revolutionary period, and faced with very difficult options could not fail to be strongly affected by external factors.

The context in which these external factors would impinge is one characterized by economic crisis. Whereas in 1974-76 there was an abundance of material on the MFA and the revolution, this optimism has largely given way to gloomy publications on the economy.[9] The World Bank report cited earlier made the point of the unfortunate timing of the Portuguese revolution. They, as do others, detail the sad aspects of the economic situation including the following: initial wage increases and productivity decreases thereby making the country's products less competitive; nationalization of banking allowing liberal credit facilities to firms on the verge of bankruptcy; fiscal system being used to provide direct subsidies to enterprises and to subsidize basic food items; exports decreasing and imports increasing; public sector deficit rising from $330 million in 1974 to $1,620 million, or 10 percent of GDP, in 1976; 1977 inflation rate of 23 percent; balance of payments upset as export receipts fall by 35 percent in real terms between 1973 and 1975; a current account surplus of $350 million in 1973 turning into deficit of $1.5 billion in 1977; and foreign currency reserves being drawn down with substantial borrowing against gold reserves.[10] The same list, maybe longer or shorter, with greater or lesser detail can be found in virtually all books on the economy. The economic situation was perilous and the country was on the verge of bankruptcy. Additionally, we must also point out that the economic problems are unlikely to be short-term and of easy resolution because of the very underdeveloped nature of the economy. Portugal has lived

off its colonies for five hundred years and this, in combination
with the economic and political system formulated by Oliveira
Salazar, has meant that the industrialization is at a rudimen-
tary level and largely noncompetitive. As this is important
both for the impact of external factors in the short-run and the
possibilities of modernization in the long-run, we must deal
with the topic briefly.

The German Development Institute divides Portugal's industrialization from the 1930s until the 1960s into two eras.[11]
Up until World War II the demand of the domestic and supple-
mentary colonial markets for simple consumer goods and
some luxury goods were met. Also, the country specialized in
the production of goods which allowed for comparative advantages arising from natural factor endowment (wines, cork, ol-
ives, sardines). The specialization in these goods did not
stimulate the development of the economy or of exports. During the second phase, World War II until the war in Angola in
1961, industries producing chiefly for the domestic market
were developed by large national companies with considerable
state assistance as part of an economic model of self-suffi-
ciency based to some extent on the colonies. Also, labor-inten-
sive consumer goods industries (textiles and clothing),
exploiting the advantages of the country's cheap labour in
comparison with other parts of West Europe, began to gear
themselves to external demand which was growing rapidly in
this era. With the wars in the colonies the country was opened
up to foreign investment, and there was a process of diversification and fairly rapid development. The diversification
touched elementary consumer-goods industries and the promotion of plants to assemble, bottle, and can imported primary
products. Also, large domestic companies, still receiving substantial state support, developed industries primarily geared
for the domestic market (mechanical engineering, transport
equipment, chemicals, etc.). "The aim of the national economic
policy was to safeguard the traditional agricultural, colonial
and power structures of the corporative system."[12] There was
indeed change and growth as could be indicated by figures on
the GDP, labor force productivity, factor endowment, and value
added.[13] However, most economists agree that the growth was
unbalanced and extremely vulnerable. As the German Development Institute describes it: "Unlike Spain, Portugal did not,
however, succeed in initiating a process of industrial development—apart from the establishment of 'scattered indus-

tries'—by opening its frontiers to the outside world.[14] Or, as
the World Bank made a similar point: "Growth was concentrated in a relatively small number of large and modern enterprises enjoying privileged access to credit and foreign
technology, while the vast majority of medium and small enterprises, accounting for the bulk of industrial employment,
were given little assistance and few incentives to modernize
and reach adequate dimensions. All this occurred in a context
of artificially low wages, low interest rates, cheap raw materials and energy, protective tariffs, and privileged conditions
for Portuguese exports in the former overseas territories."[15]

Another aspect of this vulnerability was the reliance on
remittances and tourism, sources which would be seriously
affected with recession and then revolution. In 1972 mer-
chandise exports contributed only 40 percent of total foreign
exchange inflow. Remittances from emigrants contributed 29
percent and tourism 13 percent. Obviously, the size of these remittances implied massive emigration, and indeed the population decreased by some 180,000 during the decade of the
1960s. The country's modernization strategy was obviously
not successful in absorbing the population from the stagnat-
ing agriculture.

The industrialization process, as part of a larger approach
to modernization, was not particularly enlightened or successful in Portugal. The country remained the poorest in Western
Europe with very low per capita incomes, low productivity in
most sectors, still heavily agricultural but forced to import
some 40 percent of agricultural consumption, and unable to
absorb its population growth in the small modern sectors.
With the revolution the crisis in the industrialization process,
and already in the political arena, became obvious. As the
World Bank report states it:

> "This unbalanced industrial structure proved particularly
> vulnerable to the profound changes in the domestic and in-
> ternational environment that occurred in 1974 and
> 1975.While the performance of many large firms was af-
> fected by sluggish markets, disruptions in labor relations,
> state intervention or outright nationalizations, most of the
> small and medium enterprises were plunged into a serious
> liquidity crisis by the sharp increases in nominal wages and
> in the cost of raw materials and energy. As a result, manufac-
> turing output increased by only 2% in 1974 and fell by 5% in
> 1975; manufacturing exports decreased by 10% in 1974 and

13% in 1975. The drop in profits combined with political un-
certainties caused domestic and foreign private investment
to come almost to a standstill."[16]

The most obvious and dramatic manifestation of the crisis
was the massive deficit in the balance of payments which
threatened the economic viability of the country. The deficit
was a manifestation of the structural and conjunctural problems, but also the source of other problems such as the elimi-
nation of any maneuverability internationally and the
difficulty of increasing wages and employment.[17] The less obvious but just as severe long-run manifestation of Portuguese
industrial backwardness and haphazard modernization is the
lack of competitiveness of Portuguese production.[18] The former manifestation is a useful way to enter the topic of the IMF
and investment, and the latter a good way to discuss the question of accession to the EEC.

As has been emphasized a number of times, foreign assistance played an important role in the evolution of the Portuguese political system in 1975 and 1976. Foreign states and
international institutions made suggestions, encouraged the
PS and parties to its Right to oppose the PCP, and indicated
that economic support would be forthcoming, which it was as
indicated by the figures at the end of Chapter Four. However,
by 1977 it became clear that the difficulties of the Portuguese
economy were definitely long-term and would require both
large sums of money and a certain degree of ongoing external
intervention in the economy.[19] Because of the multilateral involvement in the first place, and the desire of the principal
countries—the U.S. and the Federal Republic—to avoid too
much direct intervention, it was decided that the IMF would be
the appropriate body to deal with the problem of Portugal's
deficit. The policies and practices of the IMF are well known,
and sufficient literature exists that I need go into no detail
here.[20] As an institution with more than 130 member countries and where a "nonpolitical politics" prevails, it is extremely difficult for a country needing funds to finance a
deficit to find fault with the conditions established by the
Fund. There was some negotiation with the IMF. Judging
from my interviews and the final conditions agreed to in the
Letter of Intent, however, the PS of Mario Soares did not nego-
tiate as aggressively with the IMF as it might have.[21] In the
agreement the government committed itself to a stabilization

program to be achieved through fiscal, monetary, and wage restraint combined with an exchange rate policy. The policies included an increase in interest rates to between 18 and 23 percent, a severe restriction on credit, strict control on public sector spending to remove the deficit in the budget, elevation of certain administered prices and a limit on increases in wages, and through these measures together with general austerity bring the external account into balance. And, while it may simply be the form of these Letters of Intent, the government agreed to "take any further measures that may become appropriate for this purpose [the objectives of the program]. During the period of the stand-by arrangement, the Government will consult with the Fund on the adoption of any measures that may be appropriate at the initiative of the Government or whenever the Managing Director [of the Fund] requests consultation. . . ."[22]

My purpose in touching upon the Portugal-IMF agreement is not to denounce the Fund, for I tend to agree with the economists who indicate that similar measures would have to be taken—Fund or no Fund.[23] Rather it is to indicate that while the current accounts deficit was removed it was at the cost of a very low growth rate of some 2 percent in 1978, high unemployment, and a drop in wages.[24] That is, the macroeconomic situation which required substantial adjustment, in this case prescribed by the Fund, of necessity tightened up the domestic situation thereby removing flexibility in a whole series of economic areas from credit to costs to salaries. In short, it impinged on the approach to modernization and simply made some possibilities unviable. It should be mentioned once again that the Fund's condition of general agreement led to the collapse of the First Constitutional Government. The agreement thus had direct political implications, although I am not willing to argue that the PS governing alone was any better than the PS governing with the CDS.

If the Portugal-IMF agreement is suggestive of the constraints on Portugal at the macro level, the changing situation of regulations on direct foreign investment illustrates the same point in greater detail. We must recall that the Estado Novo did not encourage foreign investment until the mid-1960s so that although the rate increased up until 1973, the country still had the lowest level of direct foreign investment of any country in Western Europe. It is estimated that the total foreign investment in 1978 amounted to $390 million of which

50 percent was of EEC origin and 19 percent from the U.S. As Donges states,". . . Portugal accounts for a relatively small proportion of the estimated stock of foreign investment held by the highly industrialized OECD countries in the area [Southern Europe]."[25] With the revolution investment, domestic and foreign, dropped off drastically. When the First Constitutional Government took office in 1976, investment remained extremely low ($38 million in 1977–78) because of the following: continuing governmental instability, guarantees to labor enshrined in the Constitution, the undefined situation regarding indemnization, the small size of the domestic market in a Portugal without colonies, and the existence of a Foreign Investment Code passed at the same period as the Constitution (Decree-Law No. 239/76 of April 6, 1976).[26] In the various guides which evaluate the attractiveness of a country for foreign investment, Portugal ranked near to the bottom.

If the country is to develop, however, it will require substantial direct foreign investment. This is even more the case since Portugal lacks abundant natural resources and must import all of its oil. It must depend, as the German Development Institute puts it, on "a continous inflow of foreign direct investments and foreign financial aid over a long period."[27] In order to encourage this investment a Foreign Investment Institute was founded in 1977 which actively markets Portugal abroad by means of meetings, documentation, a monthly newsletter, and the promotion of new legislation. The original Foreign Investment Code was restrictive on direct foreign investment, but by now the legislation has been substantially liberalized through a series of modifications which have been introduced each year since the initial Code in 1976.[28] Donges summarizes by noting that "governments have taken measures with a view, inter alia, to restore confidence in Portugal among foreign businessmen."[29] In addition to the changes in legislation some of these measures are as follows: implementation of an economic stabilization program (IMF agreement), introduction of crawling peg exchange rate system to neutralize inflation differentials, tolerance of a decline in real wages and a widening of profit margins, a halt in nationalizations, and the promise by government that expropriated foreign investors would either be compenstated or have their properties returned. In sum, the Foreign Investment Code, in its many revisions, is indicative of the changes in atmosphere since 1976, and this, in conjunction with the above measures, suggest that the country has little option but to open itself fully if it wants economic growth. Foreign investment has indeed increased to $45 million in 1978, $85 in 1979, and $210 in 1980.

This is not the place to review all the literature on the positive or negative effects of foreign investment; indeed, the effects would appear to be mixed.[30] More importantly, this country with its small size, lack of natural resources, and present low level of development has so little negotiating ability that one must agree with the commentator on Donges paper—Rui Martins dos Santos—that the results are likely to be negative. Again, there are so few options.[31] The point here is that the Portuguese approach to modernization, as indicated by the IMF agreement or investment policies, is not determined exclusively by Portugal for the country is very severely constrained by "international realities."

This serious situation is widely recognized in Portugal, and it is for this reason that accession to the European Economic Community is seen by many as a panacea for all that ails Portugal. It will replace the colonial empire as the country's mission, its industries will absorb Portuguese workers, and its assistance will help the Portuguese to modernize in order to participate as full members in the expanded Community. Entry is supported by the socioeconomic groups and all the parties except the PCP. The sense is captured in the following quote: "having once again returned to the European fold and brought to a close a long historical cycle begun with the overseas discovery, the Portuguese are now in need of a national purpose; and in present circumstances it seems entirely natural that the search for a new destiny should lead to involvement in the process of integration in Western Europe—where Portugal belongs not only in geographical, geo-strategical and historical terms, but also on the basis of the economic realities of trade relations, capital and labor transfers."[32] The CIP, in the Congress of January 1979, called for entry as a true project of national dimensions which would bring substantial and, in their view, beneficial results for Portugal, including the following: it would serve as a means to clarify the situation of the economic system; it would have a great impact on all aspects of the economy and society; much of the legal system would have to be adjusted; and even the Portuguese political institutions would have to be adjusted in relationship with the Community.[33] And, lest we think that it is only the industrialists and members of the AD who support entry, we must recall that it was the leader of the PS, Mario Soares, who was the most active and vociferous proponent of entry. Indeed, he was prime minister in March of 1977, when the formal application for accession was made to the EEC. While visiting the Economic and Social Committee on March 12, 1977, he made the following comments:

> We have now turned towards Europe. Europe gives us the framework for development, for political democracy which is essential for the stability of the nation. If Europe were to reject our application for membership, the totalitarian movements of both the right and left which are still lurking in our country would take heart. Rejection would also adversely affect other countries such as Spain where the situation remains very confused despite the concrete moves towards democracy. . . . The Community is faced with a challenge, either to admit these European nations to its fold or to reject them on purely technical or economic grounds.[34]

Obviously this speech attempts to integrate a number of different themes, all of which amount to a panacea. The initial purpose and the haste in applying for accession in March 1977 was clearly political: a desire to ensure the continuing predominant role of the PS in this regime through the linkage with European democracies and social democratic parties. It might be noted as well that in September 1976 Portugal was admitted as the nineteenth member of the Council of Europe which, as an assemblage of democratic countries, indicated that Portugal was also democratic and linked the country further with this type of regime. The political sense of the application for accession is captured well in the following statement from the Commission of the Community: "When Greece, Portugal and Spain, newly emerging as democratic States after a long period of dictatorship, asked to be admitted to the Community, they were making a commitment which is primarily a political one. Their choice is doubly significant, both reflecting the concern of these three new democracies for their own consolidation and protection against the return of dictatorship and constituting an act of faith in a united Europe which demonstrated that the ideas inspiring the creation of the Community have lost none of their vigor or relevance. The three countries have entrusted the Community with a political responsibility which it cannot refuse, except at the price of denying the principles in which it is itself grounded."[35] The political implications for Portugal are obvious in that accession would link the country with other democratic regimes. For the Community itself accession would give a momentum, if it does not collapse completely in the process of expansion, to the Community idea and also assist in the security of Western Europe by the promotion of stable economies necessary to sustain the political democratization process in southern Europe. Apparently, Chancellor Schmidt in particular gave attention to the security perspective in encouraging the stability of southern Europe.[36] In short, most observers agree that for political reasons the accession of southern Europe, including Portugal, is good and desirable.

Portugal has been a member of the EFTA, and with the British application for accession to the EEC in 1967, negotiated an agreement with the EEC in 1972. The purpose of the agreement was for the progressive establishment of a free-trade area for industrial products between 1973 and 1977. This agreement, unlike those with other EFTA members, includes agricultural products and gave Portugal a longer adaptation period for industrial products. In January of 1976 there were further negotiations under this agreement which, in combination with the first agreement, benefited Portugal in a number of ways.[37] With the revolution, and more pointedly with the emergence of "pluralistic democracy," the EEC offered special emergency financial aid to Portugal in October 1975 of 150 million units of account and then in January of 1976 granted another 200 million units. Contacts between Portugal and the EEC are numerous, and there has been a constant procession between Lisbon and Brussels with advisors making statements while the Commission itself was carrying out its study on the Portuguese application. On April 20, 1978, the Commission sent to the Council of the EEC several documents concerning enlargement. Their opinion, though couched in a number of conditions and qualifications, is that the ". . . Community cannot leave Portugal out of the process of European integration . . . . The Commission accordingly feels that an unequivocal Yes should be given promptly to the Portuguese request to open accession negotiations as soon as possible."[38] However, in this same opinion the Commission stated that "Political considerations must not, however, be allowed to obscure the economic difficulties discussed in the following pages . . . ."[39] For the Community itself the accession poses a number of problems particularly regarding competition with Italy and France in agriculture, and the dilemma of Portuguese surplus labor in a community already faced with high levels of unemployment.[40]

Of greater concern here, however, are not the difficulties facing the Community but rather the problems posed for Portugal. Politically, at least in the short run, accession and even the process of accession has been important in consolidating a perceived link with the European democracies. Beyond this, however, and beyond what Portugal is already receiving through the agreement of 1972 and 1976, there is some question as to the concrete benefits which will arise from accession. Pitta e Cunha, for example, reported that the Commission is preparing an extraordinary program of support for Portugal. ". . . Portugal will become the recipient of real resources transferred through Community funds; moreover, it is expected that the fixing of well-defined timetables for the process of joining the Common Market will turn out to be an incentive for the highly necessary modifications in the structure of the Portuguese economy."[41] This is the key point, for the present structure of the Portuguese economy is such that it is not competitive and accession without tremendous previous changes, or massive aid, is likely to consolidate Portugal on the periphery.

Abundant and good empirical research has been carried out on the impact of EEC membership on less developed countries within the Community. The general conclusion seems to be that disparities between the richer and poorer are likely to increase rather than disappear. Klaus Esser argues, "the disparity between the leading group and the less industrialized Member States continues to grow. Especially during the economic crisis of the 70's the position of these countries (Ireland, Italy, Great Britain), which also have the most serious regional problems, has worsened as regards gross national product per capita."[42] He also shows that the corrective national and community policies and instruments have up to now proven relatively insignificant in reversing the trend. Also, the redistribution capacity of the Community's finances is limited and is likely to remain so. These findings are based on the first enlargement from a Community of six to nine. It should apply as well but more seriously to the second enlargement, and particularly to Portugal as the weakest of the three southern

European economies. For example, the per capita GDP for Portugal is only 60 percent that of Ireland, which is the least prosperous member of the Community.

As noted earlier in this chapter, the economy of Portugal is weak and production is inefficient and generally noncompetitive. There is ample material on this sad situation and little disagreement.[43] At present there is protection against imports through tariff protection, tarifflike charges, and nontariff barriers such as import surcharges and import licensing systems. With accession these forms of protection will be eliminated, and thus the medium- and small-scale industry, as well as infant industries, will be hard hit. And, given the earlier agreements with the EEC, there is little to be gained for industrial, and even some agricultural, products already enjoy free access. With accession competition will come not only from the EEC, but also some Third World countries which are exempted from customs duties through agreements such as the Lomé Convention. Therefore, "The complete opening of their markets will thus tend to perpetuate the extant typical structure of partly industrialized countries, especially in Greece and Portugal."[44]

The question now is whether the Portuguese will be able to change and reform their economy before accession lest they remain on the periphery of the modernized world from now on. Related to this is the matter of a massive infusion of Community funds to assist in this reworking of the economy. At present it looks as though some aid is forthcoming, but nothing startling. For example, in May of 1981 it was announced that 275 million units of account would be provided as preaccession assistance for six projects. This is significant, but not quite along the lines of aid being discussed in 1978 when the idea of a "solidarity plan for southern Europe" was being discussed. From what one can gather in the current difficulties of the Community, with wrangling over Britain's share of the budget, disagreements over the Common Agricultural Policy, and inflation as well as unemployment in most of the countries, it is not likely that massive assistance will be forthcoming. From reading the documents and conducting interviews with people involved in the Community, it is not possible to be sanguine about the possibilities of major assistance for Portugal with accession.[45] This being the case, it will be up to the Portuguese to define an industrial strategy within very strict lines whereby the country can change, modernize, and compete internationally without having to marginalize much of the population as has happened in some new industrializing countries of the Third World.[46] In the meantime, it is not terribly important what the precise tone of the revised Constitution is nor that the CIP have its demands implemented for expurging socialism from the Constitution. These items are simply dead letters in the context of international constraints and the internal balance of forces.

Probably the key aspect of the present balance of forces concerns the relationship between the different structures of government. In the process of constitutional revision which took place in 1981 and 1982, the most drastic changes concerned the division of power among the three organs of national government which were the Presidency of the Republic, the Revolutionary Council, and the Assembly of the Republic. Specifically they concerned the extent and balance of powers between the president and the Assembly, with particular emphasis on their roles in the formation and continuation of a government. With the exception of the PCP, no party defended the continuation of the Revolutionary Council. The crux was whether the political system remain semipresidential, or bipolar, or tend in a clearly parliamentary direction with a presumably much larger role for the political parties in the Assembly. As noted in Chapter Five the powers of the president were extensive in areas ranging from the command of the armed forces, forming and dismissing governments, vetoing legislation, and in foreign affairs. What is more, due to the failures of Constitutional Governments I–V, President Eanes utilized these powers to the fullest.[47] However, he did not institutionalize this situation through either the formation of a presidential party or revision of the Constitution on his initiative. That is, he employed the powers provided for in the Constitution but did not seek to identify them with his office or modify them for utilization under different and nonminority government situations. There were at least five proposals from a variety of politicians for the president to form his own party, revise the Constitution, and support certain candidates in the elections to the Assembly. He entertained the proposals, but remained aloof and did not provide support. The presidential orientation of the political system was thus not institutionalized but rather exacerbated in a particular conjuncture arising from the elections of April 25, 1976. This conjuncture changed radically with the interim elections of December 2, 1979, when the

AD came to power and would continue so following the elections of 1980 until the revised constitution was promulgated by President Eanes in October 1982.

From January 1980, when the Sixth Constitutional Government took office, the tensions were clear between the Aliança Democrática government on the one side and the president and Revolutionary Council on the other. The president travelled within Portugal and abroad, used the pocket veto, and the Revolutionary Council vetoed the key item in the AD program on the delimitation of economic sectors. The orientations of the president and those of the government were clearly distinct, and it is not difficult to provide evidence in this regard.[48] The resulting institutional arrangement was ambiguous: While the government, now based on a majority in the Assembly, tended to operate in a parliamentary fashion, the overall regime did not, as the president and the Revolutionary Council also enjoyed legitimacy and had broadly defined roles in the system. What is more, their orientation was more in line with the legacy of April 25, while the AD sought to change it. Tensions between the president and the government revolved around both the strategy of modernization (that enshrined in the Constitution of 1976 vs. an orientation similar to the CIP, CAP, etc.) and, more importantly, the question of power. The solution for the AD was revision of the Constitution whereby the powers of the president would be diminished and those of the government, and even the Assembly, increased.

Revision required two-thirds of the Assembly, with no veto for the president or the Revolutionary Council. However, with 134 deputies, the AD required support from another party in order to achieve the 167 necessary for revision. Thus a great deal of negotiation took place which was not restricted to the Assembly, but carried over to the parties, state apparatus, military, and the media. Revision was ultimately accomplished due to the support of Mario Soares and the Socialist Party which, together with the AD and minor parties allied with the PS, voted for revision in August 1982. The PCP voted against, and the MDP abstained. Mario Soares had promised President Eanes in the fall of 1980 that the PS would not support a constitutional revision which diminished the powers of the presidency. However, Soares has shown himself to be a flexible politician in the past and demonstrated this facility once again by supporting the revision. The president was unable to impede this process as he lacked a party, had ruled out the referendum, and had no veto. The revision which was enacted substantially changed the formal balance of powers. The result of the changes was to make the system more parliamentary and less presidential and included the following modifications: (1) The abolition of the Revolutionary Council and the creation of a Council of State which must be consulted by the president before dismissing a government or dissolving the Assembly of the Republic. Unlike the Revolutionary Council, the Council of State is composed largely of politicians and has come to include the heads of the major parties. (2) The abolition of the pocket veto and the provision that a normal veto can be overturned by a majority in the Assembly. (3) The abolition of the political responsibility of the government before the Assembly and the president and the subsequent restriction of this responsibility to the latter. (4) The appointment by the president of military commanders which are nominated by the government.[49]

Formally, in any case, the political system after revision differs substantially from its prior incarnation. In addition, the revision removed a number of the "socialistic" terms from the Constitution and somewhat modified the economic sections toward increased private involvement and greater private initiatives. Suggestive of the unrealized impact of constitutional revision is the fact that a public opinion poll administered in January 1983 disclosed that only 36 percent of those interviewed realized that the Constitution had been revised; 6 percent thought that it had not been, and 58 percent simply did not know.[50] In fact, until now the constitutional revision has not proven as crucial as many had anticipated. Potentially, it is extremely important and its implementation holds serious implications for overall regime stability and the politicization of the armed forces.[51] However, since shortly after revision in October 1982, the political system has been in a state of turbulence and confusion, a situation which has prevailed until at least mid-1983. The Eighth Constitutional Government collapsed in December due to internal problems in the AD, and particularly the PSD, and a new government could not be formed from within the AD. This necessitated interim elections to the Assembly which were held on April 25, 1983. In these elections the PS won 36 percent of the vote and 101 deputies; the PSD 27 percent and 76 deputies; the PCP 18 percent and 44 deputies; and the CDS 12 percent and 29 deputies. The remaining 7 percent were spread over 10 minor parties as well as blank and null votes. Possibly most suggestive is the fact that abstentions rose to 21 percent from 16 percent in 1980. The negotiations for forming a government took almost two months and finally resulted in a coalition between the PS and the PSD. It is premature to comment on this Ninth Constitutional Government, but it is important to note that Mario Soares sought to have as many parties, government organs, and levels of his party involved in this new government in order to broaden the base of responsibility in what are clearly perceived to be difficult economic times. In the meantime, the constitutional revisions pertaining to the distribution of powers, the nomination of the military commanders, and the economic sectors have not been fully implemented. Lacking a stable majority, in a context of governments collapsing and elections being held, it has been impossible to evaluate the impact of constitutional revision. In any case, revision has not led to political stability and the basis of power remains split between a popularly elected president, with some commitment to the goals arising from the MFA revolution, and an Assembly in which poorly integrated and unstable (save the PCP) parties with shifting orientations are predominant.

Notes

1. For very useful reviews of this topic in general see Francisco Pereira de Moura, *Por Onde Vai a Economia Portuguesa?* 4th ed. (Lisbon: Seara Nova, 1974) and Erik Baklanoff, *The Economic Transformation of Spain and Portugal* (N.Y.: Praeger, 1978).

2. On the Constitution see, in particular, Reinaldo Caldeira and Mario do Céu Silva, *Constituição Política da República Portuguesa, 1976* (Lisbon: Livraria Bertrand, 1976). On revision see, for example, A Barbosa de Melo, et. al., *Estudo e Projecto de Revisão da Constituição* (Coimbra: Coimbra Editora, Ltd., 1981). There are now two political-science type of books dealing with the political system and touching upon the revision. They are Emídio da Veiga Domingos, *Portugal Político: Análise das Instituições* (Lisbon: Edições Rolim, 1980) and Pedro Santana Lopes and José Durão Barroso, *Sistema de Governo e Sistema Partidário* (Amadora: Livraria Bertrand, 1980). On revision I interviewed in November 1981 and May 1982. For the revision, the Assembleia da República, Direção de Serviços de Divulgaçáo e Relações Públicas has published two volumes on the parties' proposed revisions, *Revisão Constitucional* (Lisbon, 15 July

1981). These have proved invaluable for a comparison of the projects with the Constitution of 1976.

3. Marcelo Rebelo de Sousa, *Direito Constitucional* (Braga: Livraria Cruz, 1979), pp. 340–41.

4. OECD, *Portugal: Economic Survey* (Paris: OECD, 1979), p. 14, reports that the real earnings per employee dropped 5 percent in 1978 and 4 percent in 1977 and are at the 1974 level. Paul Krugman and Jorge Braga de Macedo, "The Economic Consequences of the April 25th Revolution," in *Portugal Since the Revolution: Economic and Political Perspectives* eds., Jorge Braga de Macedo and Simon Serfaty (Boulder: Westview Press, 1981), pp. 74–85 show that with 1973 as 100 real wages went up to 109 in 1975 and down to 89 in 1978.

5. The weakness of the CGTP-IN was obvious in early 1982 when the general strikes called for February 12 and May 11 were fiascos. The Pope's visit in mid-May was far more effective in bringing the country to a standstill.

6. CIP, *I Congresso das Actividades Economicas* (Lisbon: CIP, 1979). The second congress was held in April 1981. See CIP, CCP, and CNAP, *II Congresso das Actividades Economicas: Sessões Plenarias & Conclusões* (Lisbon: NP, 1981). See, also, M. Belmira Martins and J. Chaves Rosa, *O Grupo Estado: Análise e Listagem Completa Das Sociedades Do Sector Público Empresarial,* (Lisbon: Edições Jornal Expresso, 1979).

7. From an English translation of the conclusions of CIP congress, p. 2.

8. Paulo de Pitta e Cunha, "Portugal and the European Economic Community," *Economia* 3 (October 1979): 526, 528. CIP, *I Congresso,* pp. 139–40.

9. See for example *The I and II International Conferences on the Portuguese Economy, 1976 and 1979* by Fundação Gulbenkian and the German Marshall Fund of the United States. Both conference proceedings in two volumes. See also *Economia* and particularly Pitta e cunha, "Portugal and the European Economic Community." The yearly OECD surveys are useful, as is The World Bank, *Portugal: Current and Economic Trends* (Washington: The World Bank, 1978).

10. The World Bank, *Portugal: Current and Economic Trends,* pp. ii–iii.

11. German Development Institute, *Portugal's Industrial Policy in Terms of Accession to the European Community* (Berlin: CDI, 1980), p. 81.

12. Ibid., p. 6.

13. See appendixes for these data.

14. GDI, *Portugal's Industrial Policy,* p. 6. See also Eric Baklanoff, "The Political Economy of Portugal's Old Regime: Growth and Change Preceding the 1974 Revolution," *World Development* 7

(1979): 799–811.

15. The World Bank, *Appraisal of Banco de Fomento Nacional: Portugal* (Washington: The World Bank, May 1977), p. 12.

16. The World Bank, *Portugal: Current and Economic Trends*, pp. 12–13.

17. On the lack of maneuverability see, Krugman and Braga de Macedo, "The Economic Consequences."

18. Of particular value on this topic is GDI, *Portugal's Industrial Policy.* A summary of the findings is Guido Ashoff, "The Southward Enlargement of the EC: Consequences for Industries and Industrial Policies," *Intereconomics* (Nov./Dec. 1980): 299–307.

19. My interviews with economic counsellors in a number of the embassies emphasized the growing awareness of the ongoing nature of the assistance and the untenable level of intervention. And the World Bank, *Portugal: Current and Economic Trends*, p.31, ". . . Portugal will continue to need large inflows of foreign capital throughout the period. This would average about $1.5 billion per annum tailing down to $1.3 billion in 1985."

20. On this see in particular Barbara Stallings, "Portugal and the IMF: The Political Economy of Stabilization," in Braga de Macedo and Serfaty, *Portugal Since the Revolution*, and the material cited there.

21 The letter of intent, in English, is a document of some 10 pages. Its conditions are described in ibid. The interview was conducted in late 1978 with an ex-minister of the PS.

22. Letter of intent, p. 9. Stallings, in "Portugal and the IMF," p. 118, indicates that it was approved by the Fund on June 12, 1978.

23. See in particular Manuel P. Barbosa and Luis Miguel Beleza, "External Disequilibrium in Portugal: 1975–78," *Economia* 3 (October 1978): 487–507.

24. OECD, *Economic Survey*, p. 5, and Krugman and Braga de Macedo, "The Economic Consequences."

25. Juergen B. Donges, "Foreign Investment in Portugal," in *II International Conference on the Portuguese Economy* (1979), p. 255.

26. See Ministry of Planning and Economic Coordination, Institute of Foreign Investment, *Foreign Investment* (Lisbon: Foreign Investment Institute, 1977).

27. GDI, *Portugal's Industrial Policy*, p. 4.

28. In addition to the Code, with all the changes until 1977, see Foreign Investment Institute, "Integrated Investment Incentive System (Decree Law no. 194/80)" (Lisbon, 1980). The Institute publishes a very useful monthly "Progress Report," a less frequent "Economic Trends Report," and an "Annual Report."

29. Donges, "Foreign Investment in Portugal," p. 258.

30. Ibid., pp. 261–70 and materials cited there.

31. Rui Martins dos Santos, "Comment on Donges," in *II International Conference*, p. 311. On specifically German investment, see

Christian Deubner, *Das Auslandskapital in der Iberischen Industrie* (Ebenhausen: Stiftung Wissenschaft and Politik, 1982).

32. Pitta e Cunha, "Portugal and the EEC," p. 513.

33. CIP, *I Congresso*, pp. 139–49.

34. EEC, Economic and Social Committee, "Dossier EXT/8 Portugal," 27 April 1977, p. 6.

35. *Bulletin of the European Communities*, Supplement 1/78, "Enlargement of the Community—General Considerations," p. 6.

36. Gunnar Nielsson and George Irani, "Greek, Spanish and Portuguese Membership of the European Communities: Prospects for States with 'Intermediate Economies'," (Paper presented to Second Conference of Europeanists, Washington, D.C., October 23–25, 1980), p. 5.

37. For the background details see, for example, *Europe Information*, "Portugal and the European Community," 7/78 (May 1978). For a positive evaluation of the results of the agreements see, for example, Arménio Cardo, *Portugal e o Mercado Comun Depois do 25 de Abril* (Lisbon: Livraria Petrony, 1976).

38. *Bulletin of the European Communities*, Supplement 5/78, "Opinion on Portuguese Application for Membership," p. 7.

39. Ibid.

40. Ibid. keeps this impact in perspective by noting that Portugal represents only 3 percent of the present Community of Nine in population and 1 percent in GDP.

41. Pitta e Cunha, "Portugal and the EEC," p. 514.

42. German Development Institute, *European Community and Acceding Countries of Southern Europe* (Berlin: GDI, 1979), p. 42.

43. See GDI, "Portugal's Industrial Policy," and Ashoff, "The Southward Enlargement of the EC."

44. Ashoff, "The Southward Enlargement of the EC," p. 305.

45. The documents include the series of the Supplements 1/78, 2/78, 3/78, 5/78, the *Europe Information, Information*. Interviews were conducted in 1978, by a colleague in 1980, and with an exmember of the Commission in 1981.

46. See the critical comments on the "orthodox strategy" by GDI, "Portugal's Industrial Policy." See, also, Beate Kohler, "Political Problems of Southward Extension," *Intereconomics* (Jan./Feb. 1979): 306, and the important book by Christian Deubner, *Der Unsichere "Europaische Konsens" in den Iberischen Landern: Der Beitritt zur EG als soziales und innenpolitisches Problem in Portugal und Spanien* (Ebenhausen: Stiftung Wissenschaft und Politik, 1981). Interestingly enough, in early 1982 some owners' groups, including the CIP, were beginning to show reservations regarding accession to the EEC. They apparently began to perceive that entry could harm their economic viability as they could not compete.

47. Santano Lopes and Durão Barroso, *Sistema de Governo*, pp. 48–73. See also Luis Salgado de Matos, "Troisieme partie," unpub-

lished Mémoire de DEA, "Le president de la Republique Portugaise dans le Cadre du Regime Politique," Université de Paris, 1 (September 1979) in two volumes.

48. See Santana Lopes and Durão Barroso, *Sistema de Governo*, pp. 80–83.

49. On the Constitution see Jorge Miranda e M. Vilhena de Carvalho, *Constituição da Republica Portuguesa: Depois da primeira revisão constituicional* (Lisbon: Rei dos Livros, 1982). For a very informed discussion on the balance of powers before and after revision see Marcelo Rebelo de Sousa, *O Sistema de Governo Português: Antes e Depois da Revisão Constitucional* (Lisbon: Cognitio, 1983).

50. See *Expresso*, 19 February 1983, pp. 31–34 R.

51. An interesting interpretation which emphasizes the importance of the revision is Joaquim Aguiar, *A Ilusão do Poder: Análise do Sistema Partidário Português, 1976–1982* (Lisbon: Publicaçôes Dom Quixote, 1983), pp. 179–82.

Conclusion

Portugal, originally one of the stronger political units in Europe and with an extensive colonial empire, was bypassed by northern Europe and particularly Great Britain from the late eighteenth century. Bypassed not only in the Industrial Revolution, but also in the democratic revolution which saw reasonably stable bourgeois democracies established in northern, if not southern, Europe. As Portugal remained on the periphery, it became increasingly consolidated and, even while continuing to hold its own colonies, remained relatively anachronistic socially and economically while dynamic processes of change transformed these other societies. Entering the twentieth century at such a low level of development, the Portuguese Republic lacked a solid sociopolitical base for the establishment of a stable regime. The instability, and indeed the nature of the parties themselves, did not create a coherent project whereby the society could be transformed. Rather, the instability led to a military coup which in turn led to the establishment of a regime which did possess a coherent, if archaic, project of economy, polity, and society.

The Estado Novo created by Premier Oliveira Salazar sought to perpetuate Portugal as an unmodern society with a colonial empire, but with minimal interactions with other, and more modern, societies. The fact that he was successful for four decades suggests something about the culture of the country as well as its level of modernization. Indeed, repression was utilized and the security apparatus extensive, but the regime ruled more by cooption than repression. And, the country was sufficiently backward that a fairly simple government—conservative and authoritarian—effectively maintained the system.

Even in Portugal this system could not have been perpetuated forever and some innovation was required. The opportunity occurred with the stroke and subsequent death of Oliveira Salazar and the coming into office of Marcello Caetano, who had been associated with, but not totally identified with, the policies of the Estado Novo. He brought promises of reform, change, and a general opening to new

145

individuals, groups, and ideas. The possibilities for change in regard to the colonies and with Portugal's relations with Europe were discussed, as were development plans within Portugal itself. However, for a number of reasons, including Caetano's personality, the power bloc established by Oliveira Salazar, and the weakness of an opposition, his reforms were not implemented. Rather, Portugal under Caetano had the worst of all possible combinations: unmodern but with some obvious aspects of change necessary, and committed to retaining the colonies despite the fact that they were an increasing burden. In the face of demands for change both nationally and in its relations with other countries, the regime became paralyzed. Within the country the reaction was obvious as evidenced by strikes, demonstrations, and general discontent, which was met with increased repression. The manifestations would amount to a crisis in society, which penetrated the military as well and took the form of meetings, statements, and finally plotting. The decision to overthrow the regime was made, however, for largely military reasons: professional career problems and, most importantly, the realization that the wars could not be won militarily. As the regime was intransigent in all respects, there was no option but to overthrow it since not even the highly regarded General Spínola could bring about change.

The overthrow, or more accurately, the collapse of the Estado Novo opened the way to any number of possible regimes and paths to modernization. In the Portuguese revolution of 1974–76 most of the options previously implemented, or even contemplated, were discussed with an eye to experimenting with them in Portugal. The problem was, however, that there was no single group with power which also possessed a coherent project for modernization. Power became dispersed throughout the armed forces and the parties, and it was impossible for any group to implement its model of modernization. Thus while a great variety of changes did in fact take place at all levels of economy and society, these were not made according to any particular, well-considered project. Rather, they took place due to the collapse of the old system, the competition for power among groups and parties, and the very dynamic of this struggle in which the people also became haphazardly involved. Thus Portugal changed, but not according to any plan.

tial elections in 1985. The approach to modernization being discussed today by the PS has little to do with its Program in the summer of 1976 when it formed the First Constitutional Government.

Politics, however, is not the only process involved in defining the Portuguese approach to modernization. The people's attitudes and activities suggest that there is great leeway for almost any government, provided it is sufficiently distanced from the revolution. The population is disgruntled with many of the results of the revolution and is unlikely to oppose a government seeking to dismantle many of the changes.

Portugal, even with the colonies, was a weak country. Today, without the colonies, with the haphazard changes, with conjunctural problems of recession and energy costs, the country is fragile indeed. This is obvious in macroeconomic terms, decisions on investment, and regarding specific sectors of commerce and industry. In this serious situation the accession to the European Economic Community has been seen as something of a panacea which will guarantee democracy, modernize the country, and bring in wealth and stability. Politics applies as well to the EEC and while there may be some leeway, at the present it would appear that the promise of accession is greater than the results are likely to show. The mere fact of lack of modernization means that entry, without a great deal of unlikely assistance, will affect the country adversely and place Portugal in an economic position worse than before 1974. Thus accession, if not done in the most careful terms possible, may well further consolidate Portugal on the periphery and preclude its participation in a beneficial way in processes and trends of the modern world. It must be noted, however, that by early 1982 the CIP, originally among the most fervent supporters of accession, has now reconsidered its views as the economic realities of full membership are better understood.

The large questions are now being determined through politics. Portugal possesses a political system in which the interests and concerns of the population can be represented through elections and groups. The options, however, are quite limited both domestically and internationally, and it is probably just as well that by allowing all to participate, all are in some way responsible. Thus while the conditions allowing for modernization are now present, the country has a long way to

Conclusion

Due to the interaction of elements within the arme
an initial commitment to elections, the emergence of
parties, and foreign pressures, there was established
1975 the possibility of a liberal democratic regime.
gime did in fact emerge by mid-1976 due to the st
among groups and parties, and specific pressure app
number of foreign actors. Thus although the pattern
ernization remained to be defined, there was at least tl
lishment of a political system in line with the MFA 1
and the orientations of the major political parties. Th
cal system, however, represented, as it probably ha
legacy of two years of revolution in which the instituti
defined rather to the Left and in which the Constitu
shrined many of the changes brought about in the
two years. Further, the PS coming to power represen
its opposition to the PCP and the favored links betwee
and important foreign actors.

The type of political system established by n
served to effectively institutionalize uncertainty by
structures and processes whereby a variety of actors
a variety of resources could promote their own goals a
ests. Thus despite the fact that the PS did possess a p
modernization, as seen in their Programa do Governo
not hold all power in the system. Indeed, with a minor
Assembly, and considering the weight of the issues t
fronted, it is little wonder that the government c
within a year and a half. What this implied, however,
other political groups and parties, with their own ap
to modernization, could counter that promoted by the
institutional situation which emerged from the rise c
in 1979 pitted the president, until revision in 1982 v
port of the Revolutionary Council, against the gove
Politics came to concern not only short-term gaining
and the interaction of personalities and parties, but
approach to modernization that the country was to ad
stitutional revision changed the formal arrangement
and also opened the way to redefining much in the
and society. However, just as the PS could not hold on
from mid-1977 so the AD collapsed and the PSD cou
turn, retain power from late-1982. Now in mid-1983 t
previously antagonistic parties, the PS and the PSD,
to form a "central bloc" and possibly govern until the

go before they are fulfilled. In the meantime a great deal depends on the capacity and concerns of the political elites. As Oliveira Salazar was able to form a regime which guaranteed the survival of an anachronistic society, it now remains to be seen whether the present elite can form a regime guaranteeing the formation of a modern society.

Appendix I

Basic Statistics: International Comparisons

	Reference period	Units	Belgium	Canada	France
Population	Mid-1977	Thousands	9,830	23,316	53,084
Inhabitants per sq. km.	»	Number	322	2	96
Net average annual increase	Mid-1967 to Mid-1977	%	0.3	1.3	0.7
Employment: Total civilian	1977	Thousands	3,711	9,754	20,884
of which: Agriculture, forestry, fishing	»	% of total	3.3	5.7	9.6
Industry[4]	»	»	37.9	28.9	37.7
Other	»	»	58.8	65.4	52.7
Gross Domestic Product at market prices	1977	US $ billion[11]	79.2	200.3	380.7
Average annual volume growth[6]	1972 to 1977	%	3.2	4.2	3.3
Per capita	1977	US $[11]	8,060	8,590	7,170
Gross Fixed Capital Formation	1977	% of GDP	21.2	22.7	22.6
of which: Transport, machinery and equipment	»	»	6.4	7.6	
Residential construction	»	»	7.1	6.0	7.5
Average annual volume growth[6]	1972 to 1977	%	2.9	4.5	1.5
National Savings Ratio[12]	1977	% of GNP	21.7	21.3	23.4
General Government					
Current expenditure on goods and services	1977	% of GDP	17.3	20.3	14.9
Current transfer payments	»	»	22.0	12.4	24.8
Current revenue	»	»	41.8	36.4	42.2
Net Official Development Assistance	1977	% of GNP	0.5	0.5	0.6
Indicators of Living Standards					
Private consumption per capita	1977	US $[11]	5,000	4,870	4,450
Passenger cars, per 1,000 inhabitants	1976	Number	279	388[20]	300
Telephones, per 1,000 inhabitants	»	»	300	596	293
Television sets, per 1,000 inhabitants	1975	»	255	411	268
Doctors, per 1,000 inhabitants	»	»	1.9	1.7	1.5
Access to higher education[15]	»	% of relevant age group	34.4[16]	49.8[13]	31.4[16]
Infant mortality[12]	»	Number	14.6	15.0[16]	12.6
Wages and Prices	Average annual increase				
Hourly earnings in industry[18]	1972 to 1977	%	15.4	12.5	15.7
Consumer prices	»	%	9.7	8.9	10.3
Foreign Trade					
Exports of goods, fob	1977	US $ million[11]	37,488[7]	41,556	63,516
As percentage of GDP	»	%	47.2	21.1	16.7
Average annual volume increase	1972 to 1977	%	4.8	3.7	6.3
Imports of goods, cif	1977	US $ million[11]	40,248[7]	39,540	70,488
As percentage of GDP	»	%	50.7	20.1	18.5
Average annual volume increase	1972 to 1977	%	5.8	5.4	5.5
Total Official Reserves	End-1977	US $ million	5,761[7]	4,608	10,194
As percentage of imports of goods	In 1977	%	14.3[7]	11.7	14.5

1. Partly from national sources.
2. Total resident population.
3. Private and socialized sector.
4. According to the definition used in OECD: Labour Force Statistics: mining, manufacturing, construction and utilities (electricity, gas and water).
5. Social product.
6. At constant prices.
7. Including Luxembourg.
8. Excluding ships operating overseas.
9. Fiscal year beginning April 1st.
10. 1973.
11. At current prices and exchange rates.
12. $\left| \dfrac{\text{GNP} - (\text{Priv. cons.} + \text{Pub. cons.})}{\text{GNP}} \right| \times 100.$
13. 1972.
14. 1976.
15. Figures are not strictly comparable due to differences in coverage. For more details see "Educational Statistics Yearbook - Volume I (1974) and volume 2 (1975) - OECD, Paris".
16. 1974.
17. Deaths in first year per 1,000 live births.
18. Figures are not strictly comparable due to differences in coverage.
19. Private.
20. 1975.
21. 1971 to 1976.

150

Germany	Greece	Ireland	Italy	Nether-lands	Portugal	Spain	Switzer-land	Turkey	United Kingdom	United States
61,400	9,268	3,180	56,446[2]	13,853	9,773	36,672	6,327	42,135	55,919	216,817
247	70	45	187	410	106	73	153	54	229	23
0.4	0.6	0.9	0.7	1.0	0.7	1.1	0.4	2.5	0.2	0.9
24,488	(3,167)	1,022	19,847	4,555	3,781	12,462	2,817	14,151	24,550	90,546
6.8	(28.4)	23.1	15.9	6.3	32.5	20.7	8.5	55.8	2.7	3.6
45.3	(30.3)	30.3	38.6	33.2	33.1	37.4	42.7	13.6	40.0	(28.9)
47.9	(41.3)	46.6	45.5	60.5	34.4	41.9	48.8	30.6	57.3	(67.5)
516.2	26.2	9.4	196.1	106.4	16.3	115.6	60.6	44.8	244.3	1,878.8
2.3	3.8	3.2	3.0	3.0	3.8	3.7	−0.5	7.2	1.8	2.6
8,410	2,830	2,940	3,470	7,680	1,670	3,150	9,580	1,170	4,370	8,670
20.9	23.0[8]	24.7	19.8	21.1	20.4	21.5	20.7	25.8	18.1	17.5
8.3	8.4	14.7	8.5	8.6	5.5[14]	8.9[14]	6.9		9.0	7.3
5.9	7.1	14.0	5.5	5.8	2.8[14]			3.7	3.3	4.8
−1.1	−1.4	1.8	−0.2	0.9	1.6[21]	3.7	−5.0	10.3	0.6	0.3
24.2	19.9	17.0	22.1	23.5	11.0	20.2	26.5	17.2	20.3	17.7
20.0	15.9	18.6	14.0	18.3	14.0	10.3	12.9	14.5	20.8	18.4
19.5	11.6	13.3	22.7	30.9	15.8[14]	12.7	15.3	9.2	13.9	11.6
43.5	29.4	35.6	37.7	54.0	28.3[14]	26.7	34.3	21.6	40.0	32.0
0.3			0.1	0.9			0.2		0.4	0.2
4,690	1,890	1,900	2,220	4,480	1,260	2,180	6,100	810	2,580	5,600
308	55	175	283	273	107	148	281[20]	11	255	505
343	238	150	271	391	119	237	634	28	394	721
306	126	192	213[16]	259[16]	65	184	273	12[16]	320	571[16]
2.0	2.0	1.2	2.1	1.6	1.3	1.8[14]	1.8	0.6	1.3	1.6
24.2[16]			31.0	21.1[16]	(9.8)[10]	29.3[10]			21.8[16]	43.2
15.7	24.1	18.4	20.7	10.6	37.9[16]	18.9	10.7		16.0	16.1
8.7	23.2	20.0	24.4	12.0	17.5	23.2	5.8	27.5	16.5	8.1
5.7	16.1	16.1	16.5	8.7	21.1	16.6	5.6	30.0	16.3	7.7
117,936	2,724	4,392	45,036	43,680	2,028	10,223	17,544	1,753	57,516	120,168
22.9	10.6	47.7	23.0	41.1	11.9	8.8	28.7	3.9	23.5	6.4
6.7	11.3	9.0	6.1	5.4	1.8	8.6	5.9	1.8	6.7	6.4
100,704	6,780	5,388	47,556	45,600	4,956	17,835	17,904	5,796	63,696	147,852
19.6	26.3	58.6	24.3	42.9	29.2	15.4	29.3	12.9	26.1	7.8
5.5	5.1	6.3	1.4	3.8	3.4	3.8	1.5	8.7	3.1	4.5
39,737	1,020	2,372	11,629	8,065	1,377	6,590	13,830	630	21,057	19,390
39.5	15.0	44.0	24.5	17.7	27.8	36.9	77.2	10.9	33.1	13.1

Note: Figures within brackets are estimates by the OECD Secretariat.

Sources: Common to all subjects and countries: OECD: Labour Force Statistics, Main Economic Indicators, National Accounts, Observer, Statistics of Foreign Trade (Series A); Office Statistique des Communautés Européennes, Statistiques de base de la Communauté; IMF, International Financial Statistics; UN, Statistical Yearbook.

Source: *Portugal*, OECD Economic Surveys; July 1979.

Selective Bibliography

Aguiar, Joaquim. *A Ilusão do Poder: Análise do Sistema Partidário Português, 1976–1982.* Lisbon: Publicações Dom Quixote, 1983.

Almeida, Diniz. *Ascensão, Apogeu e Queda do MFA.* Lisbon: Edições Sociais, 1977? n.d.

———. *Origens e Evolução do Movimento de Capitaës.* Lisbon: Edições Sociais, n.d.

Álvares, Pedro, and Carlos Roma Fernandes. *Portugal E O Mercado Comum: Dos Acordos de 1972 as Negociações de Adesão.* Lisbon: Editorial Portico, 1980.

Antunes, Albertino, Alexandre Manuel, António Amorim, and Mário Bacalhau. *Portugal: República Socialista?* Amadora: Heptágono, Estudos e Publicações, SARL, 1975.

Antunes, Albertino, Alexandre Manuel, António Amorim, et al. *A Opção Do Voto.* Lisbon: Intervoz, Publicidade, Limitada, 1975.

Antunes, Ministro Mél, Francisco S. Cabral, César de Oliveira, et al. (contributors). *Debate Sobre O Programa De Política Económica e Social.* Lisbon: Moraes Editores, 1975.

A revolução das flores: do 25 de Abril ao Governo Provisorio. 2.ª edição. Lisbon: Editorial Aster, n.d.

A revolução das flores: O governo de Vasco Gonçalves até ao Acordo de Lusaka. Lisbon: Editorial Aster, n.d.

Ashoff, Guido. "The Southward Enlargement of the EC: Consequences for Industries and Industrial Policies," *Intereconomics* (November/December 1980): 299–307.

Assembleia da República, Direcção de Serviços de Divulgação e Relações Públicas. *Revisão Constitucional.* 2 vol. 1981.

Atlas Eleitoral. Lisbon: Editorial Progresso Social e Democracia, SARL, 1981.

Augusto Seabra, José. *Portugal Face à Europa (Um Horizonte Cultural).* Porto, Athena, 1977.

Bacalhau, Mário. *Inquérito A Situação Política: Eanes A Solução?* Lisbon: Heptágono, Estudos e Publicações, SARL, n.d.

Baklanoff, Eric N. "The Political Economy of Portugal's Old Regime: Growth and Change Preceding the 1974 Revolution." *World Development* 7 no. 8/9 (1979): 799–811.

Balso, Judith. *Compasso Do Tempo: O M.R.P.P.* Lisbon: Edições Delfos, n.d.

Banco de Portugal. *1975–1980 Indicadores Económicos: Portugal.* Lisbon: Banco de Portugal, 1981.

Bandarra, Álvaro, and Nelly Jazra. *A Estrutura Agrária Portuguesa Transformada?* Lisbon: Iniciativas Editoriais, 1976.

Barbosa de Melo, A., J.M. Cardoso da Costa, and J.C. Vieira de Andrade. *Estudo e Projecto De Revisão Da Constituição.* N.P.: Coimbra Editora, LDA, 1981.

Barreto, Antonio. *Pour Une Réforme Agraire Démocratique et Constitutionnelle.* N.P.: Ministre de l'Agriculture et des Peches, 1977.

Barão da Cunha, Manuel. *Radiografia Militar.* Lisbon: Editorial O Século, 1975.

Barros, Afonso. *Reforma Agrária em Portugal.* Oeiras: Fundação Gulbenkian, 1979.

Barros, Henrique. *Ainda e Sempre A Reforma Agrária.* N.P.: Ministério da Agricultura e Pescas, 1977.

———. *A Estrutura Agrária Portuguesa.* N.P.: Editorial República, 1972.

Barroso, Alfredo. *Portugal: A Democracia Dificil.* N.P.: Grafica Bras Monteiro, LDA., 1975.

Bell, Coral. *The Diplomacy of Detente: The Kissinger Era.* New York: St. Martin's Press, 1977.

Belmira Martins, Maria, and J. Chaves Rosa. *O Grupo Estado: Análise e Listagem Completa Das Sociedades Do Sector Público Empresarial.* Lisbon: Edições Jornal Expresso, 1979.

Belmira Martins, Maria. *Sociedades e Grupos Em Portugal.* Lisbon: Editorial Estampa, 1975.

Blackburn, Robin. "The Test in Portugal." *New Left Review* 87–88 (September-December 1974): 5–46.

Blume, Norman. "Portugal Under Caetano." *Iberian Studies* 4 (Autumn 1975): 46–52.

———. "Sedes: An Example of Opposition in a Conservative Authoritarian State." *Government and Opposition* (Summer 1977): 351–66.

Braga de Macedo, Jorge, and Simon Serfaty (eds.). *Portugal Since the Revolution: Economic and Political Perspectives.* Boulder: Westview Press, 1981.

Brito, Rui de. *Anatomia Das Palavras: Vasco Gonçalves.* Lisbon: Liber Documento, 1976.

Bruce, Neil. *Portugal: The Last Empire.* London: David & Charles, 1975.

Bruneau, Thomas C. "Church and State in Portugal: Crises of Cross and Sword." *Journal of Church and State* (Autumn 1976).

————. *Os Portugueses e a Política Quatro Anos Depois do 25 de Abril.* In conjunction with Mário Bacalhau. Lisbon: Editorial Meseta, 1978.

————. "Out of Africa into Europe: Towards an Analysis of Portuguese Foreign Policy." *International Journal* 32 (Spring 1977): 288–314.

————. "Patterns of Politics in Portugal Since the April Revolution." In *Portugal Since the Revolution: Economic and Political Perspectives,* edited by Jorge Braga de Macedo and Simon Serfaty. Boulder: Westview Press, 1981.

————. "Portugal in the 1970s: From Regime to Regime." *Ibero-Amerikanisches Archiv* (Berlin) (January 1982).

————. "Portugal: Problems and Prospects in the Creation of a New Regime." *Naval War College Review* 29 (Summer 1976).

————. "The Left and the Emergence of Portuguese Liberal Democracy." In *Eurocommunism and Eurosocialism: The Left Confronts Modernity,* edited by Bernard E. Brown. New York: Cyrco Press, 1979.

Burchett, Wilfred. *Portugal Antes e Depois do 25 de Novembro.* Lisbon: Seara Nova, 1976.

————. *Portugal Depois da Revolução dos Capitães.* Lisbon: Seara Nova, 1975.

Cabral, Francisco Sarsfield. *Uma Perspectiva Sobre Portugal.* Lisbon: Moraes Editores, 1973.

Caetano, Marcello. *Constituições Portuguesas.* Lisbon: Editorial Verbo, 1978.

————. *Depoimento.* Rio de Janeiro: Distribuidora Record, 1974.

————. *Manual De Direito Administrativo.* Lisbon: Coimbra Editora, Limitado, 1973.

————. *Minhas Memórias De Salazar.* 2nd ed. Lisbon: Editorial

Verbo, 1977.

Calafate, Tenente-Coronel, Luís. *A Liberdade Tem Um Preço*. Póvoa de Varzim, 1975.

Caldeira, Reinaldo, and Maria do Céu Silva. *Constituição Política da República Portuguesa 1976*. Lisbon: Livraria Bertrand, 1976.

Campinos, Jorge. *Ideologia Política Do Estado Salazarista*. Lisbon: Portugális Editora, n.d.

––––––. *O Presidencialismo do Estado Novo*. Lisbon: Perspectivas & Realidades, 1978.

Cándido de Azevedo, J. *Portugal Europa Face Ao Mercado Comum*. Amadora: Livraria Bertrand, 1978.

Cardo, Arménio. *Portugal e o Mercado Comum Depois Do 25 de Abril*. Lisbon: Livraria Petrony, 1976.

Carvalho, Joaquim Barradas. *O Obscurantismo Salazarista*. Lisbon: Seara Nova, 1974.

Castro, Armando de. *O Pensamento Económico no Portugal Moderno (De fins do século XVIII a começos do século XX)*. Instituto De Cultura Portuguesa, Ministério Da Cultura e Da Ciencia, Secretaria De Estado Da Cultura. Amadora: Livaria Bertrand, 1980.

Castro, Armando de, A.J. Avelás Nunes, Joaquim Gomes, and V. Tribuna Moreira. *Sobre O Capitalismo Português*. Coimbra: Atlântida Editora, 1974.

Cavaco Silva, Aníbal A. *A Política Económica do Governo de Sá Carneiro*. Lisbon: Publicações Dom Quixote, 1982.

Commission of the European Communities Spokesman's Group and Directorate-General for Information. "Portugal and the European Community." *Europe Information, External Relations* 34/80 (Brussels: 1980).

Commission of the European Communities Spokesman's Group and Directorate-General for Information. "Portugal and the European Community." *Europe Information, External Relations* 7/78 (Brussels: 1978).

Commission of the European Communities. "Enlargement of the Community: Economic and Sectoral Aspects." *Bulletin of the European Communities*. Supplement 3/78, 1978, Belgium.

––––––. "Enlargement of the Community: General Considerations." *Bulletin of the European Communities*. Supplement 1/78, 1978, Belgium.

––––––. "Enlargement of the Community: Transitional Period and Institutional Implications." *Bulletin of the European Communities*. Supplement 2/78, 1978, Belgium.

―――. "Opinion on Portuguese Application for Membership." *Bulletin of the European Communities*. Supplement 5/78, 1978, Belgium.

Confederação da Indústria Portuguesa. *I Congresso Das Actividades Económicas*. Lisbon: C.I.P. 1979.

―――. *II Congresso Das Actividades Económicas*. Lisbon: C.I.P. 1979.

Conflict Studies. "Portugal: Revolution and Backlash." no. 61, September 1975.

Constituição da República Portuguesa. Lisbon: Rei dos Livros, 1977.

Constituição da República Portuguesa: Depois da primeira Revisão Constitucional. Verificação do texto e notas de Jorge Miranda e M. Vilhena de Carvalho. Lisbon: Rei dos Livros, 1982.

Cordeiro, René A. "Recent Evolution and Development Prospects of Portuguese Industry." Paper presented in New York on 27 October 1980.

Crollen, Luc. *Portugal, the U.S. and NATO*. Louvain: Leuven University Press, 1973.

Cunhal, Álvaro. *A Revolução Portuguesa: O Passado e o Futuro*. Lisbon: Editorial Avante, 1976.

Cutileiro, José. *A Portuguese Rural Society*. Oxford: The Clarendon Press, 1971.

da Costa, Ramiro. *O Desenvolvimento De Capitalismo Em Portugal*. Lisbon: Assirio & Alvim, 1975.

Domingos, Emídio da Veiga. *Portugal Político: Análise das Instituiçoes*. Lisbon: Edições Rolim, 1980.

Donges, Juergen B., et al. *The Second Enlargement of the European Community: Adjustment Requirements and Challenges for Policy Reform*. Tubingen: JCB Mohr, 1982.

Donges, Juergen B. "Industrial Development and Competitiveness in an Enlarged Community. Paper prepared for the conference on Portugal and the Enlargement of the European Community. 24–26 January 1980, Lisbon.

"Dossier" Carlucci/CIA. Lisbon: Editorial Avante, 1978.

"Dossier" Eleições: Em Que Sentido se Desloca O Eleitorado Português? Lisbon: Edições Avante, 1977.

Durão Barroso, José. "Les formes et les temps politiques de la démocratisation: le cas portugais." April 1982. Mimeographed.

———. "Quelques éléments pour l'étude des partis politiques portugais: organisation; clivage idéologique; bibliographie sélective. November 1982. Mimeographed.

Esser, Klaus, Guido Ashoff, Ansgar Eussner, and Wilhelm Hummen. *Portugal's Industrial Policy in Terms of Accession to the European Community.* Occasional Paper Number 60, German Development Institute (GDI), (Berlin: 1980).

Esser, Klaus, Hans Gsanger, Christian Heimpel, et al., *European Community and Acceding Countries of Southern Europe.* Occasional Papers of the German Development Institute, no. 54, Berlin: 1979.

Faye, Jean Pierre, ed. *Portugal: The Revolution in the Labyrinth.* London: Spokesman Books, 1976.

Fernandes, Capitão. *Portugal: Nem Tudo Está Perdido: do Movimento dos Capitães ao 25 de Novembro.* Lisbon: Biblioteca Ulmeiro n. ⁰1, 1976.

Ferrâo, Carlos. *História da la República.* Lisbon: Terra Livre, 1976.

Ferreira, Serafim (Coordenação). *MFA Motor Da Revolução Portuguesa.* Lisbon: Diabril Editora, 1975.

Figueiredo, Antonio de. *Portugal: Fifty Years of Dictatorship.* Middlesex: Penguin Books, 1975.

Fisher, H.E.S. "Anglo-Portuguese Trade 1700–1770. In *The Growth of English Overseas Trade in the Seventeenth and Eighteenth Centuries,* edited by W.E. Minchinton. London: Methuen & Co., 1969.

Fonseca Ferreira, António. *A Acumulação Capitalista Em Portugal: Das origens da nacionalidade aos inícios do seculo xix.* Porto: Edições Afrontamento, 1977.

Frémontier, Jacques. *Portugal . . . les points sur les i*(Paris: Editions Sociales, 1976).

Fryer, P., and P.M. Pinheiro. *Oldest Ally: A Portrait of Salazar's Portugal.* London: D. Dobson, 1961.

Fundação Calouste Gulbenkian and the German Marshall Fund of the United States. *2ª Conferência Internacional Sobre Economia Portuguesa, 26 a 28 Setembro 1979.* 2 vols. Lisbon: 1980.

Gallus, Georg. "Agricultural Problems of the Accession of Greece, Portugal and Spain to the EC." *Intereconomics* (January/February 1979): 6–10.

Gaspar, Jorge, and Nuno Vitorino. *As Eleições De 25 De Abril: Geografia E Imagem Dos Partidos.* Lisbon: Libros Horizonte, LDA, 1976.

German Marshall Fund of the United States and Fundação Calouste Gulbenkian. *Conferência Internacional Sobre Economia Portuguesa, 11 a 13 de Outubro de 1976.* 2 vols. Lisbon: 1977.

Gomes, Paulino, and Tomás C. Bruneau. *Eanes: Porque o Poder?* Lisbon: Intervoz, 1976.

Gonçalves, Vasco. *Discursos, Conferencias de Imprensa, Entrevistas.* Porto: Edição Popular, 1976.

Gonzalez Hernandez, and Juan Carlos. "El proceso electoral portugués. Análisis cuantitativo del comportamiento politico (1975–1976)." *R.E.O.P.* no. 48 (1977): 205–70.

Governo Provisório Da República Portuguesa. *Programa De Política Económica E Social.* Lisbon: 1975.

Graham, Lawrence S. *Portugal: The Decline and Collapse of an Authoritarian Order.* Beverly Hills: Sage Publications, 1975.

Graham, Lawrence S., and Harry M. Makler, (eds.). *Contemporary Portugal: The Revolution and Its Antecedents.* Austin: University of Texas Press, 1979.

Graham, Lawrence S., and Douglas L. Wheeler, (eds.). *In Search of Modern Portugal: The Revolution and Its Consequences.* Madison: University of Wisconsin Press, 1983.

Green, Gil. *Portugal's Revolution.* New York: International Publishers, 1976.

Harsgor, Michael. "Portugal in Revolution." *The Washington Papers,* vol. 3, no. 32. Beverly Hills and London: Sage Publications, 1976.

Harsgor, Michael. *Naissance d'un Nouveau Portugal.* Paris: Editions du Seuil, 1975.

Harvey, Robert. *Portugal: Birth of a Democracy.* London: The Macmillan Press Ltd., 1978.

Heady, Earl O. *Análise Do Desenvolvimento Agrícola e Da Reforma Agrária Em Portugal.* N.P.: Ministério Da Agricultura e Pescas, 1977.

Hermassi, Elbaki. *The Third World Reassessed.* Berkeley: University of California Press, 1980.

Holland, Stuart. "Dependent Development: Portugal as Periphery." In *Underdeveloped Europe: Studies in Core-Periphery Rela-*

tions, edited by Dudley Seers, et al. Sussex: Harvester Press, 1979.

Insight Team of the Sunday Times. *Insight on Portugal: The Year of the Captains.* London: André Deutsch Limited, 1975.

Institute of International Studies. "Portugal and Spain: Transition Politics." Essay Series, no. 5. University of South Carolina, Columbia, South Carolina: May 1976.

Instituto de Estudos Para O Desenvolvimento. "Problemas Relacionados Com A Adesão De Portugal à C.E.E.: Estratégias e Conceitos." Caderno 2. Lisbon: 1981.

Instituto Português De Opinião Pública e Estudos De Mercado. *Os Portugueses e a Política—1973.* Lisbon: Moraes Editores, 1973.

Joxe, Alain. "Le mouvement des forces armées Portugaises." *Politique Etranger* 39 (1974): 659–87.

Keefe, Eugene K., et al. *Area Handbook for Portugal.* Washington, D.C.: Government Printing Office, 1977.

Kohler, Beate. "Political Problems of the Southward Extension." *Intereconomics* (January/February 1979): 3–5.

Kolm, Serge-Christophe. "Chili-Portugal: Vers une théorie des processus révolutionnaires modernes." *Annales Economies, Sociétés, Civilisations* 31 (novembre-décembre 1976): 1245–61.

Kramer, Heinz. "Lagenotiz: Zur Situation in Portugal Zu Beginn Der Beitrittsverhandlungen Mit Der Europaischen Gemeinschaft." Stiftung Wissenschaft und Politik, Forschungsinstitut Für Internationale Politik Und Sicherheit, SWP-LN 2203, Fo. Pl. I.2A/78, Februar 1979.

Kramer, Jane. "A Reporter at Large: The Portuguese Revolution." *The New Yorker,* December 15, 1975, pp. 92–131.

Lamounier, Bolivar. "Notes on the Study of Re-Democratization." Working Paper no. 58, The Wilson Center, Latin American Program. Washington. D.C.: n.d.

Lopes, Pedro Santana, and José Durão Barroso. *Sistema De Governo e Sistema Partidário.* Amadora: Livraria Bertrand, 1980.

Lourenço, Eduardo. *O Fascismo Nunca Existiu.* Lisbon: Publicações Dom Quixote, 1976.

———. *Os Militares e O Poder:* Lisbon: Editora Arcádia, SARL, 1975.

Lourenço, Cap. Vasco. *MFA: Rosto De Povo.* Lisbon: Portugália Editora, no. 9, n.d.

Lucena, Manuel. *A Evolução do Sistema Corporativo Português: I O Salazarismo*. Lisbon: Perspectives & Realidades, 1976.

————. *A Evolução do Sistema Corporativo Português: Il O Marcelismo*. Lisbon: Perspectives & Realidades, 1976.

————. *O Estado Da Revolução: A Constituição de 1976*. Lisbon: Edições Jornal Expresso, n.d.

Lurdes Lima Santos, Maria de, Marinús Pires de Lima, and Vítor Matias Ferreira. *O 25 De Abril e As Lutas Sociais Nas Empresas*, 2 vols. (Porto: Edições Afrontamento, 1976).

Mailer, Phil. *Portugal: The Impossible Revolution?* London: Solidarity, 1977.

Makler, Harry. "The Portuguese Industrial Elite and its Corporative Relations: A Study of a Compartmentalisation in an Authoritarian Regime." *Economic Development and Cultural Change* 24 (April, 1976).

Marcum, John. "Portugal and Africa: The Politics of Indifference." Maxwell School of Citizenship and Public Affairs, *Eastern African Studies* 5 (March 9, 1972).

Martins, Almeida, Cáceres Monteiro, and João Vaz. *Por Onde Vai Portugal?* Amadora: Jornal do Fundão Editora, 1975.

Martins, Herminio. "Opposition in Portugal." *Government and Opposition* 4 (Spring 1969): 250–63.

————. "Portugal." In *European Fascism*, edited by S.J. Wolf. London: Weidenfeld and Nicolson, 1968.

Martins Pereira, João. *O Socialismo: A Transição e O Caso Português*. Amadora: Livraria Bertrand, 1976.

Matias Ferreira, Vitor. *Da Reconquista Da Terra à Reforma Agrária (as ocupações de terras no Alentejo)*. Lisbon: A Regra do Jogo, edições, 1977.

Maxwell, Kenneth. "The Emergence of Portuguese Democracy." In *From Dictatorship to Democracy: Coping with the Legacies of Authoritarianism and Totalitarianism*, edited by John H. Herz. Westport, Conn.: Greenwood Press, 1982.

————. "The Thorns of the Portuguese Revolution." *Foreign Affairs* 54 (1976): 250–70.

McGovern, George. *Revolution into Democracy: Portugal After the Coup*. Washington, D.C.: U.S. Government Printing Office, 1976.

Medeiros Ferreira, José. *Do Código Genético No Estado Democrático.* Lisbon: Contexto Editora, LDA., 1981.

Medeiros Ferreira, José. *Ensaio Histórico sobre a Revolução do 25 de Abril.* Lisbon: Imprensa Nacional–Casa da Moeda, 1983.

————. *Manifesto Reformador.* Apresentado Ao Pais Em 18 de Abril de 1979, N.P.

Mercadante, Paulo. *Portugal Ano Zero.* Rio de Janeiro, editora artenova, s.a., 1975.

Middlebrook, Kevin J. "Prospects for Democracy: Regime Transformation and Transitions From Authoritarian Rule." Working Paper no. 63, The Wilson Center, Latin American Program, Washington, D.C.: n.d.

Middlemas, Keith. *Cabora Bassa: Engineering and Politics in Southern Africa.* London: Weidenfeld and Nicolson. 1975.

Miranda, Jorge. *Constituição e Democracia.* Lisbon: Livraria Petrony, 1976.

Modesto Navarro, António. *Vida ou Morte no Distrito de Viseu.* Lisbon: Prelo Editora, SARL, 1976.

Moore, Barrington, Jr. *Social Origins of Dictatorship and Democracy: Lord and Peasant in the Making of the Modern World.* Boston: Beacon Press, 1967.

Moreira Alves, Marcio. *Les soldats socialistes du Portugal* (Paris: Editions Gaillimard, 1975).

————. *Os Soldados Socialistas de Portugal.* Lisbon: Iniciativas Editoriais, 1975.

Mota, José Gomes, *A Resistência: O Verão Quente de 1975.* Lisbon: Edições Expresso, 1976.

Mujal-Leon, Eusebio. "The PCP and the Portuguese Revolution." *Problems of Communism* 26 (January-February 1977): 21–41.

Manuela de S. Rama, M., and Carlos Plantier. *Melo Antunes: Tempo de Ser Firme.* Lisbon: Liber, 1976.

Murteira, Mário. *Textos De Política Económica.* Lisbon: Serv. Sociais Dos Trabalhadores DA C.G.D. Secção Cultural, 1975.

Nogueira Pinto, Jaime. *Portugal Os Anos Do Fim: De Goa Ao Largo De Carmo,* vol. 2. N.P.: Sociedade de Publicações Economia & Finanças, LDA, 1977.

Nogueira Pinto, Jaime. *Portugal: Os Anos Do Fim: A Revolução Que Veio De Dentro.* N.P.: Sociedade De Publicações Economia &

Finanças, LDA, 1976.

Oliveira Marques, A.H. *History of Portugal.* 2nd ed., 2 vols. New York: Columbia University Press, 1976.

Oliveira, César. *M.F.A. e Revolução Socialista.* 2.ª edição. Lisbon: Diabril Editora, 1975.

Opello, Walter. "Portugal." In *Political Parties of Europe,* edited by Vincent McHale. N.Y.: Greenwood Press, forthcoming.

Opello, Walter C., Jr. "Local Government and Political Culture in a Portuguese Rural County." *Comparative Politics* 13 (April 1981): 271–89.

———. "The Parliament in Portuguese Constitutional History." *Iberian Studies* 7 (Spring 1978): 22–29.

———. "The Second Portuguese Republic: Politico-Administrative Decentralization Since April 25, 1974." *Iberian Studies* 7 (Autumn 1978): 43–48.

Organization for Economic Co-operation and Development. *Portugal.* Paris: OECD, 1981, 1979, 1977, 1976.

Partidos e Movimentos Politicos em Portugal. Braga: SOAPLI, Sociedade De Estudos e Publicações, LDA, 1975.

Payne, Stanley G. *A History of Spain and Portugal.* 2 vols. Madison: University of Wisconsin Press, 1973.

Pereira de Moura, Francisco. *O Projecto Burguês Do Governo Socialista.* Lisbon: Seara Nova, 1977.

———. *Por Onde Vai A Economia Portuguesa?* 4th ed. Lisbon: Seara Nova, 1974.

Pereira Gil, L. *Novembro 25: Anatomia De Um Golpe.* Lisbon: Edição Editus, 1976.

Pimlott, Ben. "Parties and Voters in the Portuguese Revolution: The Elections of 1975 and 1976." *Parliamentary Affairs* 30 (Winter 1977): 35–58.

———. "Portugal—Two Battles in the War of the Constitution." *West European Politics* 4, May 1, 1981, pp. 286–96.

———. "Socialism in Portugal: Was it a Revolution?" *Government and Opposition* 12 (Summer 1977): 332–50.

Porch, Douglas. *The Portuguese Armed Forces and the Revolution.* London: Croom Helm, 1977.

Programa Do Governo: Apresentação Para Apreciação Debate Encerramento Do Debate. Lisbon: 1976.

Przeworski, Adam. "Some Problems in the Study of the Transition to Democracy." Working Paper Number 61, The Wilson Center, Latin American Program. Washington, D.C.: n.d.

Rafael, Franciso, Jorge B. Preto, Maria Ana Casanova, et al. (trabalho colectivo). *Portugal/Capitalismo e Estado Novo: Algumas Contribuições Para O Seu Estudo.* Porto: Edições Afrontamento, 1976.

Rebelo de Sousa, Marcelo. *Direito Constitucional. I - Introdução à Teoria da Constituição.* Braga: Livraria Cruz, 1979.

―――. *O Sistema de Governo Português: Antes e Depois da Revisão Constitucional.* Lisbon: Cognitio, 1983.

Ribeiro, Sérgio. *A Adesão Ao Mercado Comum: Fatalidade ou Opção?* Lisbon: Seara Nova, 1977.

―――. *O Mercado Commum: A Integração e Portugal.* Lisbon: Editorial Estampa, 1976.

Robinson, Richard. *Contemporary Portugal: A History.* London: George Allen & Unwin, 1979.

Rodrigues, Avelino, Cesário Borga, and Mário Cardoso. *Abril nos Quartéis de Novembro.* Lisbon: Livraria Bertrand, 1979.

―――. *O Movimento dos Capitães e o 25 de Abril: 229 Dias para Derrubar O Fascismo.* Lisbon: Moraes Editores, 1974.

―――. *Portugal Depois de Abril.* Lisbon: Intervoz, 1976.

Roma Fernandes, Carlos, and Pedro Alvares. *Portugal e o Mercado Comum.* Lisbon: Moraes Editores, 1972.

Rosa, Eugénio. *A Economia Portuguesa Em Numeros.* Lisbon: Moraes Editores, 1975.

Rui Vilar, Emílio, and António Sousa Gomes. *Sedes: Dossier 70/72.* Lisbon: Moraes Editores, 1973.

Salazar, Oliveira. *Como se Levanta um Estado* (Prefacio de Jorge Morais). Lisbon: Golden Books, 1977.

Salgado de Matos, Luis. *Le President de la République Portugaise dans le cadre du regime politique.* Mémoire de D.E.A., elaboré sous la direction de M. Maurice Duverger, Université de Paris I, Département de Science Politique de la Sorbonne, septembre 1979.

Santa-Ritta, Gonçalo. *Portugal: Agricultura E Problemas Humanos.* Lisbon: Terra Livre, 1979.

Saraiva de Carvalho, Otelo. *Alvorada em Abril.* Amadora: Livraria Bertrand, 1977.

————. *Cinco Meses Mudaram Portugal.* Lisbon: Portugália Editora, 1975.

Saraiva, José António. *Do Estado Nova à Segunda República: Crónica Política de um Tempo Português.* Amadora: Livraria Bertrand, 1974.

Schmitter, Philippe C., and Gerhard Lehmbruch, eds. *Trends Towards Corporatist Intermediation.* Beverly Hills: Sage Publications, 1979.

Schmitter, Philippe C. *Corporatism and Public Policy in Authoritarian Portugal.* Beverly Hills: Sage Publications, 1975.

————. "Liberation by Golpe: Retrospective Thoughts on the Demise of Authoritarian Rule in Portugal." *Armed Forces and Society 2* (November 1975): 5–33.

Sideri, S. *Trade and Power: Informal Colonialism in Anglo-Portuguese Relations.* Rotterdam: Rotterdam University Press, 1970.

Silva Lopes, Victor. *Constituição Da República Portuguesa 1976 (anotada).* N.P.: Edição Editus, n.d.

Silva Martins, J. *Estruturas Agrárias Em Portugal Continental.* 2 vols. Lisbon: Prelo Editora, 1975.

Skocpol, Theda. *States and Social Revolutions: A Comparative Analysis of France, Russia and China.* New York: Cambridge University Press, 1979.

Soares, Mário, Willy Brandt, and Bruno Kreisky. *Liberdade Para Portugal.* Amadora: Livraria Bertrand, 1976.

Soares, Mário. *Portugal Amordaçado: Depoimento sobre os anos do Fascismo.* N.P.: Editora Arcádia, 1974.

————. *Portugal: Que Revolução?* Lisbon: Perspectivas & Realidades, 1976.

Spínola, António. *Ao Serviço de Portugal.* Lisbon: Atica/Bertrand, 1976.

————. *Portugal e O Futuro.* N.P.: Editora Arcádia, SARL, 1974.

Stepan, Alfred. *The State and Society: Peru in Comparative Perspective.* Princeton: Princeton University Press, 1978.

Sousa Ferreira, Eduardo. *Estruturas De Dependência.* Lisbon: Iniciativas Editoriais, n.d.

Sweezy, Paul M. "Class Struggles in Portugal." *Monthly Review 27* (September 1975): 1–38.

————. "Class Struggles in Portugal - Part 2." *Monthly Review* 27 (October 1975): 1–15.

Szulc, Tad. "Lisbon and Washington: Behind the Portuguese Revolution." *Foreign Policy* 21 (Winter 1975–76): 3–62.

Tavares-Teles, António. *Otelo.* Lisbon: 18 de janeiro editora, 1976.

Tsoukalis, Loukas. *The European Community and its Mediterranean Enlargement.* London: George Allen & Unwin, 1981.

Urban, Joan Barth. "Contemporary Soviet Perspectives on Revolution in the West." *Orbis* 19 (Winter 1976): 1359–1402.

U.S. Congress. Senate. Subcommittee on Foreign Assistance of the Committee on Foreign Relations. *Military and Economic Assistance to Portugal.* Washington, D.C.: U.S. Government Printing Office, February 25, 1977.

U.S. Congress. Senate. *Portugal in Transition.* A report to the Committee on Foreign Relations prepared by Mike Mansfield. Washington, D.C.: U.S. Government Printing Office, September 1975.

U.S. Congress. Senate. *Portugal (Including the Azores) and Spain in Search of New Directions.* A report to the Committee on Foreign Relations prepared by Claiborne Pell. Washington, D.C.: U.S. Government Printing Office, March 1976.

Valente, Vasco Pulido. *Estudos Sobre a Crise Nacional.* Lisbon: Imprensa Nacional, 1980.

Wallraff, Gunter. *A Descoberta De Uma Conspiração: A Acção Spínola.* Lisbon: Livraria Bertrand, SARL, 1976.

Wheeler, Douglas L. "Days of Wine and Carnations: The Portuguese Revolution of 1974." *New Hampshire Council on World Affairs Bulletin* 20 (July 1974).

————. *Republican Portugal: A Political History 1910–1926.* Madison: The University of Wisconsin Press, 1978.

Wiarda, Howard J. *Corporatism and Development: The Portuguese Experience.* Amherst: University of Massachusetts Press, 1977.

————. "Spain and Portugal." In *Western European Party Systems,* edited by Peter H. Merkl. New York: The Free Press, 1980.

World Bank. *Appraisal of Banco de Fomento Nacional Portugal.* Report no. 1462a-PO, 1977.

————. *Portugal: Agricultural Sector Survey.* Washington, D.C.: The World Bank, 1978.

————. *Portugal: Current and Prospective Economic Trends.* Washington, D.C.: The World Bank, 1978.

Newspapers

Expresso for the period 1974–82.

O Jornal for the period 1976–80.

Consultation of complete clipping files for the following newspapers for those parts of the period 1974–80 during which they were published.

A Capital	*Jornal Novo*
O Dia	*A Luta*
O Diário	*Movimento*
Diário de Lisboa	*República*
Diário de Notícias	*O Século*
Jornal do Comércio	*O Tempo*

Index

About the Author

Thomas C. Bruneau received his PhD in Political Science from the University of California at Berkeley in 1970. Since that time he has been teaching at McGill University in Montreal where he was also director of the Centre for Developing Area Studies between 1978 and 1983. In 1983 and 1984 he is the Senior Program Associate in the Latin American Program of the Wilson Center in Washington, D.C. Dr. Bruneau has researched extensively in Brazil and has published two books and a dozen articles on that country. His most recent book is The Church in Brazil: The Politics of Religion (Austin: The University of Texas Press, 1982). He has been researching in Portugal since 1973 and has published nine scholarly articles and co-authored one book (in Portuguese) on politics in that country. Dr. Bruneau is currently working on a new research project on the political system in Portugal and will conduct field research there in 1984.